WORKING

WITH AGENCIES

An Insider's Guide

WORKING
WITH AGENCIES

An Insider's Guide

MICHAEL SIMS

John Wiley & Sons, Ltd

Published by   John Wiley & Sons Ltd, The Atrium, Southern Gate, Chichester,
West Sussex PO19 8SQ, England

Telephone (+44) 1243 779777

Email (for orders and customer service enquiries): cs-books@wiley.co.uk
Visit our Home Page on www.wiley.com

Other Wiley Editorial Offices

John Wiley & Sons Inc., 111 River Street, Hoboken, NJ 07030, USA

Jossey-Bass, 989 Market Street, San Francisco, CA 94103-1741, USA

Wiley-VCH Verlag GmbH, Boschstr. 12, D-69469 Weinheim, Germany

John Wiley & Sons Australia Ltd, 33 Park Road, Milton, Queensland 4064, Australia

John Wiley & Sons (Asia) Pte Ltd, 2 Clementi Loop #02-01, Jin Xing Distripark, Singapore 129809

John Wiley & Sons Canada Ltd, 22 Worcester Road, Etobicoke, Ontario, Canada M9W 1L1

Wiley also publishes its books in a variety of electronic formats. Some content that appears
in print may not be available in electronic books.

British Library Cataloguing in Publication Data

A catalogue record for this book is available from the British Library

ISBN-13 978-0-470-02461-4 (HB)
ISBN-10 0-470-02461-5 (HB)

Typeset in 12/16pt Bembo by Laserwords Private Limited, Chennai, India
Printed and bound in Great Britain by Antony Rowe Ltd, Chippenham, Wiltshire
This book is printed on acid-free paper responsibly manufactured from sustainable forestry
in which at least two trees are planted for each one used for paper production.

To all those clients who take the leap of faith

CONTENTS

INTRODUCTION   xi

ACKNOWLEDGEMENTS   xiii

**1   AGENCIES: CAN'T LIVE WITH THEM, CAN'T LIVE
     WITHOUT THEM**   3

Understanding What you Want from an Agency   5
Understanding the Nature of your Organization   8
The Collaborative Spirit: The Essential Ingredient   13
Starting off on the Right Foot   16
Ensuring that the New Team Works Well Together   19

2   HOW AN AGENCY WORKS BEHIND THE SCENES   27

Understanding how an Agency is Structured   28
   Client Services   29
   Senior Management   33
   Account Planning   34
   The Creative Team   35
   Media/Data   37
   Creative Services   38
   Artwork Studio/Digital Production   38

Finance		39
Understanding the Creative Development Process		40
Strategic Planning		41
Campaign and Creative Briefings		42
Concept Development		42
Concept Execution		42
Production/Distribution		44
3	**SELECTING AN AGENCY**	**47**
Preparation Before an Agency Review		49
Working with Third-Party Specialists		54
Guidelines on Agency Search and Selection		56
Meeting the Agency Face-to-Face		68
Post-Pitch Feedback		70
4	**BRIEFING AN AGENCY**	**75**
The Value of the Briefing Process		76
The Role of the Different Briefing Stages		77
The Key Elements to the Brief		79
Four Principles for a Good Brief		80
Understanding the Brand		81
Achieving Clarity		82
Maintaining Focus		83
Creating Surprise		83
The Hotspots of the Brief		84
The Objective of the Communications		85
The Customers		85
The Proposition and Support		87
Developing a Challenging Communications Proposition		87
Creating an Inspiring Briefing		91
5	**CHAMPIONING THE CREATIVE PRODUCT**	**95**
How to Evaluate Creative		96

Preparing the Groundwork	96
Determining your Evaluation Criteria	97
Establishing the Right Mindset	102
Providing Usable Feedback	106
Creating a Creatively Receptive Environment	108
Presenting Creative Effectively	109

6   SMOOTHING THE WAY FOR EFFECTIVE CAMPAIGNS — 117

Establishing Project Management Systems	118
Clarity of Goals and Roles	118
Project Management Team	119
Project Management Procedures	120
Project Administration	121
Project Status Communications	122
Internal Communications	122
Approval Procedures	124
Checking the Legal Aspects	125
Moving from Concepts to Campaign Execution Effectively	127
Managing Problems with a Creative Concept	128

7   TAKING CARE OF THE FINANCES OF THE RELATIONSHIP — 135

Different Agency Remuneration Structures	136
Commission	136
Phased Fee	137
Project Fee	139
Payment by Results	139
Working with Procurement	140
Contract or No Contract?	143
Setting a Budget	144
How an Agency Works in Terms of Finances	145
Campaign Budgeting	147

Issuing an Accurate Campaign Estimate   149
Invoicing   151
Final Reconciliations   153

8   DEVELOPING A LONG-TERM RELATIONSHIP   159

Managing Creativity   160
Knowing the Friction Points   164
    Costs   164
    Time   164
    Creative Amends   165
    Production   166
    Attitude   166
Balancing Success and Failure   167
Getting your Portfolio of Agencies to Work Together   167
Evaluating Agency Performance   170
    Defining the Agency Role and its Service Levels   171
    Creating Evaluation Procedures   172

EPILOGUE   181

REFERENCES   183

USEFUL INFORMATION SOURCES   185

ABOUT THE AUTHOR   187

INDEX   189

INTRODUCTION

Working with Agencies springs from the work I have recently been doing with client companies helping them to work more effectively with their agency partners. Clients understand their own organizations and their marketing needs very well but they can often regard agencies as a 'black box of mysterious arts' or as 'a necessary evil'. Yet, they are dependent on agencies to help them to produce outstanding marketing communications. If you are a client of an agency, you will want to set the pace for the relationship. This handbook provides guidelines, practical tips and techniques for those who need to get the most from an agency relationship, whether they have been working with agencies for some time or have just started. Companies who understand how agencies really operate and how to work with them effectively can reap the benefits. They will achieve strong marketplace presence, an efficient way of working and, ultimately, the essential associated business results.

We are seeing a transition in how clients and agencies want to work together though I would say that three core ingredients for a productive partnership remain – knowledge, trust and a sense of collaborative adventure. This *Insider's Guide* seeks to examine the relationship from both sides and identifies how clients can achieve these three key ingredients when selecting an agency, briefing campaigns and developing work.

Working with Agencies is designed for all levels in marketing departments and also for those who have the role of managing agency relationships. It is not specific to one sector and it relates to dealing with agencies of any type which produce a creative product. Therefore the common activity could be sales promotion, design, brand advertising, PR, event management, digital media or direct marketing. I draw on my own experiences, joint industry guidelines, anecdotal evidence from clients and agencies, research into what makes such relationships tick, plus tried and tested training material that has found appeal with companies such as bmi, BUPA, Ericsson, Ford, Lloyds TSB and Xerox.

In our daily lives, we encounter so many examples of marketing mediocrity. This book will help you to create or enhance a relationship where you can avoid such mediocrity. Moreover, not only will you derive immense personal satisfaction from striving together with your agency for that excellence, but you will give your company the best possible chance to make the desired market impact.

HOW TO READ THIS BOOK

In developing the book, I have been conscious that there is very little spare time for those in business to read vast tracts of text. The format has been established to help different levels and those with specific interest areas: it can be read like a novel from start to finish or it can be used like a Haynes Motor Manual to guide you through tricky situations.

Each chapter is peppered with specific tips, comments and anecdotes. At the beginning of each chapter, there is a list of what you will cover and at the end there is a list of short exercises that will help you to analyse your own situation better.

ACKNOWLEDGEMENTS

· ·

I have drawn on a variety of sources for inspiration and have acknowledged my gratitude by quoting them where appropriate. You will also find a complete listing of the reference literature in the Appendix.

In particular, I would like to thank the IPA, ISBA, MCCA, PRCA and the DMA for their help and permission to reproduce some of their guidelines at various points in the book. I would like to express my thanks to AAR and Express Train for being able to draw on findings from their client/agency research. As I wanted to show recent case studies and methodologies, I would like to thank Partners Andrews Aldridge and BUPA, Lexus, Lloyds TSB and the Art Fund for their cooperation.

I would also like to express my gratitude to a long list of individuals who made this book possible: Steve Aldridge, Phil Andrews, Leslie Butterfield, Matt Button, Jill Bentley, Sarah Christie-MacAllan, Sarah Ciccone, Julie Constable, Iain Dawson, Rebekah Farr, Peter Field, Kerry Glazer, Chris Gottlieb, Mathew Gully, Mark Hanson, Sarah Heard, Karen Humphreys, Nina Jasinski, Martin Jones, Carolyn Jordan, Spencer McHugh, Lyn McQueen, Esther Markham, Ian Massey, Shaun Moran, Debbie Morrison, Dominic O'Neil, Hamish Pringle, Phil Rolfe, Julie Sabin, Clare Simpson, Scott Wackett, Paul Walton and Kate Waters. This list does not include my family and all the other friends who gave their moral support in the completion of the book. They definitely deserve my gratitude.

Thank you also to those at John Wiley & Sons Ltd who brought this to fruition.

AGENCIES: CAN'T LIVE WITH THEM, CAN'T LIVE WITHOUT THEM

CHAPTER 1

AGENCIES: CAN'T LIVE WITH THEM, CAN'T LIVE WITHOUT THEM

In this chapter you will learn about:

- Understanding what you want from an agency.
- Understanding the nature of your organization.
- The collaborative spirit: the essential ingredient.
- Starting off on the right foot.
- Ensuring the new team works well together.

Just read the marketing press on one single day; it is difficult to understand what the norm currently is in agency–client relationships. Our world is full of stories of clients and their agencies either having created breakthrough campaigns or failing to spark off each other and going their separate ways. Some companies lead and manage agencies, some agencies drag their clients kicking and screaming into the white heat of creative adventure in the hope of potential business results. We could read one year that the latest phone company is pushing the boundaries of customer communications with its advertising and PR agencies, the next we read it is bitching about the same agencies and looking for replacements. Yet, you could cite the longstanding examples of Ford and Imagination, The Economist and AMV.BBDO, Tesco and EHS Brann among others. So, why is there such great diversity? Surely you would think that everyone is looking for the same thing? And, if there is no norm, does this mean that we cannot learn anything for our own circumstances and relationships?

To answer the last point first, I am convinced that there is a lot to learn for our own circumstances despite this diversity. Both clients and agencies are still looking for a mutually beneficial partnership but things have slightly altered. My view is that in the client–agency relationship, we have been undergoing a change of the model in the last 15 years which has resulted in fragmented structures. In addition (since this book deals with those relationships of any agency discipline), it has become clear that the different disciplines, although they have a creative product in common, operate on different business models and in different client contexts. Hence more fragmentation. In fact, we always had complexity: the fact that companies, agencies and market sectors were so different meant that there was always this diversity of relationship.

Juxtaposed against this backdrop, the last few years have seen clients and agencies becoming more experienced and both sides adopting a more confident, practical approach. Both sides are hungry for a new way of working. What it has meant is that now there are better opportunities for partnership if both sides get it right.

Sure, it is always going to be difficult to regard the ideal client–agency relationship as one of real equitable purity for the very reason that one of the parties will always initiate the relationship, pay for the other's services and terminate things when it is desirable. This will undoubtedly affect how both parties view each other and their ensuing existence together. However, I believe it is possible to structure how you work with an agency so that both you and the agency feel that you are reaping the rewards of a mutually beneficial partnership.

As the agency's client, you need to set the pace. In order to achieve the rewards of collaboration, you need to decide what you are looking for from the agency and how your company/marketing department can prepare and maintain the ground accordingly. Obviously you may be working with a number of agencies, therefore your task will be more complex but the same principles will still apply. What follows are the steps to help you to build a strong platform with your agency by understanding the dynamics of your own operations and matching them to what the agency can best deliver.

UNDERSTANDING WHAT YOU WANT FROM AN AGENCY

You might think that if you are a campaign manager in a UK-based company working with an agency, you would be looking for things very different from the global marketing director of IBM. In fact there are a lot of similarities in the basic elements, it is just that each company will put emphasis and priorities on different things according to their product, market operations, scale and routes to market.

Both the campaign manager and the global marketing director would recognize the following statements:

> 'I want an agency that can get the results we need.'
> 'I want an agency that understands my complex company and is willing to think on my behalf and put my company at the centre of the agency's priorities.'
> 'I want an agency to demonstrate a good return on marketing investment.'
> 'I want an agency which both thinks and executes well.'
> 'I want impactful, creative communications.'
> 'I want an agency to come in on budget and on time and never give me nasty surprises.'
> 'I want a down-to-earth agency I can trust to deliver.'
> 'I want an agency that understands my company and my marketplace and can help me with my wider business issues.'
> 'I want an agency to work well with our other departments and agencies.'

In essence, what your company and many others are looking for is an agency that can deliver:

- understanding of the business issues.
- marketplace knowledge.
- accountability.
- excellent strategic thinking.
- excellent creative expression and implementation.
- cultural/chemistry fit.

- geographical coverage.
- marketing vision.
- world-class people.
- solutions which integrate with your other activities.

Compare this with what agencies want out of the relationship:

> *'I want a profitable client for whom we can do outstanding work.'*
> *'I want a client who will become our partner and work with us.'*
> *'I want a client who takes risks and helps us produce award-winning work.'*
> *'I want a client who understands our business, how we make money and how we can work best together.'*
> *'I want a client who knows what is wanted but is willing to be surprised.'*
> *'I want a client who enhances our reputation and inspires us to do great work.'*

In summary, agencies are looking for an inspirational partner delivering:

- Spirit of partnership and involvement.
- Client profitability and growth.
- Emphasis on creativity.
- Understanding of agency environment.
- Inspiring marketing vision.
- Enhancement of the agency brand through association.
- Ease of working.

Research for AAR (conducted by Express Train in 2002 and 2003) revealed that there was a growing importance among clients for agencies to work professionally, flexibly and accountably as like-minded business partners delivering in an integrated environment rather than as creatively precious mavericks. Incidentally in the same research, when agencies were asked to define the barriers to better client relationships, lack of access to senior people and an attendant feeling of being undervalued and under-rewarded were at the top of the blame list. This was followed by the perceived consequences of working with junior clients, poor briefs and communication and a breakdown of trust. (Ouch! – Do not worry – we will be pursuing this opposing dynamic throughout the chapters.)

At this stage, what is important is knowing that you and your agency will be looking for different things from the relationship, which will allow you to develop the partnership on an axis of mutual benefit and consensual understanding. Consequently it may be worth analysing your existing agency from the criteria just discussed to enable you to see whether you are in a position to achieve this mutuality. I will explore this type of evaluation further in Chapter 3, 'Selecting an Agency', when dealing with incumbent agency problems but have a look at the scoring matrices in Figures 1.1 and 1.2. These are examples of a local marketing agency which creates design work for a client's retail outlets, but you can use the templates for yourself by identifying your key criteria, prioritizing them and seeing how you and your agency score.

Your criteria	Your level of importance	Agency score	Comment
Understanding of business issues	4	4	Good understanding of business goals, company operations, politics, personalities, etc.
Marketplace knowledge	3	3	Knows trends at local level but does not have strong sector knowledge. OK for us to provide this
Strategic thinking	4	3	Good implementing. Could be better strategically
Creative expression/implementation	4	3	Concepts can be very samey
Cultural fit/chemistry	4	4	Very good day-to-day team
Marketing vision	5	3	Agency management does not provide this
World-class people	5	4	Day-to-day contacts excellent on implementation side but lacking vision
Integration with other agencies	5	4	We determine this
Results	5	4	Outlets are happy with material provided. Market results not directly trackable

(Scoring 1–5: 1 = very low, 5 = very high)

Figure 1.1   Sample evaluation criteria matrix: you on your agency

COMMENT

In the local marketing agency example, the client has scored the agency well overall, but what comes over is that although the agency is very good both on the internal/political side and on local knowledge, it lacks heavyweight

Agency criteria for clients working with agencies	Your assessment of their rating of importance	How you think your company rates	Your comments
Spirit of partnership and involvement	5	4	At campaign manager level this is stronger. Could be better at senior level
Understanding of agency	4	3	We need to get closer to them
Emphasis on creativity	3–4	3	Creativity gets downplayed with the logistics
Inspiring marketing vision	3	4	We provide this to other agencies but it feels like more an implementation task with these guys
Client profitability and growth	5	5	We are their biggest client!
Brand enhancement	4	4	We enhance their reputation
Ease of working	5	3–4	This could be better

(Scoring 1–5: 1 = very low, 5 = very high)

Figure 1.2   Sample evaluation criteria matrix: what you think the agency thinks about you

senior involvement and creative excellence. So there is room for improvement. Interestingly, however, in Figure 1.2 the client identifies the root causes of some of the issues raised in the agency evaluation: it looks as though he/she is saying that the agency is not given the exposure to his/her company's senior management and marketing vision. Also by measuring the direct impact of the communications, the client might have a better method of benchmarking. By just making sure you complete both matrices and put yourself in the agency's shoes, you may be able to highlight not only what importance you give to certain elements of the relationship with your agency, but you may also be able to see some of the existing shortfalls from another angle.

Equally, if you are starting out with a new agency or have not worked with agencies before, Figure 1.1 will help you to determine what you are looking for and the weighting by which you will be judging any new encounter.

UNDERSTANDING THE NATURE OF YOUR ORGANIZATION

It is all very well to imagine that certain companies want excellent creativity and certain agencies want to be partnered rather than 'supplier managed', but this partnership can only really function in a practical context. Also, it is very simplistic to think that 'nimble' FMCG companies can push the strategic boundaries and pursue exciting creative work while 'sober' business-to-business companies should not attempt such heights. One of the best collaboratively creative accounts I have ever worked on was an automotive engineering operation, marketing to engineers and technicians. You must determine what is right for your circumstances and consider how you can maximize that in your agency relationship. Recently, one of my clients felt that it could be getting more out of the agency relationship, so it took a hard look at itself and what made up its existing working practices. The areas it looked at could easily form the basis of how you evaluate your own situation. Below are the questions we developed for the internal interviews:

- How could you describe the company culture? (See list of adjectives in Figure 1.3)
- How would you describe the marketing department?
- What areas of campaign development do you rely on agencies to fulfil?
- What are the most important day-to-day skills in the department?
- Are there areas of campaign development you need external help with?
- What areas do you feel should be fulfilled by your marketing department?
- How confident is your team in the areas of:

  1 Understanding the business/communication issues?
  2 Understanding agencies?
  3 Working with other departments/partner companies?
  4 Briefing and creative evaluation?
  5 Project managing?
  6 Evaluating campaign costs?

- What are the areas that you would prioritize for improvement?
- How could your agencies help in these areas of improvement?

TIP

You can probably answer all these questions yourself, but if you have already identified certain issues that exist, you may want to canvas your team or department for their answers as it will give you a more representative picture. It may also highlight areas of issue/improvement not only to you but to your colleagues. You could ask your agency or another department to answer some of the same questions to enable you to see how many external perceptions of your working

academic	down-market	international	reserved
active	down-to-earth	inviting	robust
ageless	dreamy	irresistible	romantic
agreeable	dull	jolly	sad
aggressive	dynamic	kind	scheming
angry	easy-going	lazy	secretive
amusing	elderly	leisurely	self-assured
approachable	elegant	level-headed	selfish
artistic	enterprising	lively	sensitive
aristocratic	exciting	loyal	serene
assured	exclusive	majestic	serious
attractive	exotic	manly	sexy
authoritarian	experienced	masculine	shallow
bad-tempered	extravagant	mature	sham
beautiful	extrovert	mean	show-off
boisterous	fair-minded	middle-aged	showy
bold	fatherly	middle-class	shrewd
boring	fashionable	mild	simple
bright	firm	miserly	slick
broad-minded	flamboyant	moody	smart
budget-conscious	forceful	naïve	smooth
businesslike	fresh	narrow-minded	snobbish
busy	friendly	neat	sophisticated
calculating	frivolous	nervous	sporty
calm	fussy	obliging	status-conscious
careful	generous	ordinary	stimulating
charming	gentle	ostentatious	stolid
cheeky	genuine	out-of-date	strong
cheerful	glamorous	overdressed	successful
classic	glowing	overwhelming	superior
clean	go-ahead	pale	sympathetic
coarse	greedy	patient	traditional
cold	grudging	patriotic	tranquil
cool	gullible	peaceful	trend-setting
colourful	happy	persuasive	trendy
comfortable	has-been	phoney	trustworthy
complicated	haughty	pious	unbending
composed	heavy-handed	pleasant	unchanging
concerned	high-class	polished	understanding
condescending	honest	polite	uneducated
confident	hospitable	popular	unique
conservative	hot	posh	unsociable
conventional	image-conscious	powerful	untamed
cultured	imaginative	predictable	unusual
deceitful	immaculate	presumptuous	up-market
deep-thinking	immature	pretentious	vain
deliberate	impersonal	primitive	warm
determined	impressive	professional	wealthy
devious	independent	proud	welcoming
different	individual	quiet	well-known
distinctive	inspiring	recognized	wise
distinguished	intelligent	relaxed	worldly
down-at-heel	interesting	reliable	youthful

Source: Phil Rolfe, 1827 consulting, London 2004

Figure 1.3   Selection of adjectives describing individuals or departments

practices there are. Remember to approach it with your team the right way. Handled wrongly, it may come over as a witch-hunt or, even worse, as one of those blue-suited business consultant's audits!

COMMENT

In the disguised examples in Figures 1.4 and 1.5, it is interesting to see how people in a department describe themselves. 'Business-like', 'welcoming' and 'professional' are the three most popular descriptions. In this particular organization, they define themselves as very 'warm and friendly' and with a strong work ethic. However what I have noticed in similar organizations is that sometimes this sociability and business-like nature does not necessarily mean that everything is in order. Sometimes departments can be very sociable but they do not share campaign learnings, etc. Also if it is a hard-working team, sometimes, as the song goes, they are so 'heads down, no-nonsense mindless boogie' that they get fixated on the processes rather than the quality of the outcome.

In the day-to-day skills assessment, in Figure 1.5, if you were the department head of this company you would need to ask whether 'understanding customer needs' and 'market knowledge' was too peripheral in the skill set at present. It may be that other departments supply these for you. I would also reiterate that 'organizational skills' gives the marketing department a feel that they are more process-oriented than focused on the outcome.

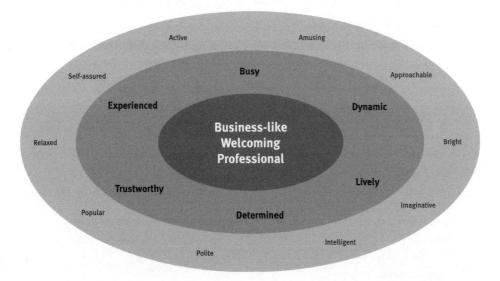

Figure 1.4 How members of a marketing department might describe themselves within the company

Figure 1.5 How members of a marketing department might describe their essential day-to-day skills

Another way of understanding how your department works and what reliance you want on an agency is a GAP analysis. You assess what you need to deliver as a marketing department and what is missing from your internal resources, and thereby you identify what you need to commission from agencies (and/or other departments) and whether your culture and teams are geared to work with agencies in the best way.

Figure 1.6 presents an example of such a GAP analysis for a business-to business requirement.

Communications delivery findings	Requirements
• Main communication activities are – Direct marketing to niche market – Liaison with trade press • Communications strategy determined by other department • Strong reliance on agencies • Strong brand • Dependence on creative product • High frequency of campaigns	• DM and PR agencies • Implementation agencies required • Understanding of how agencies work • Brand knowledge in agencies and campaign teams • Established benchmarks in creative process • Good project management skills

Figure 1.6 Sample capability requirement gap analysis

THE COLLABORATIVE SPIRIT: THE ESSENTIAL INGREDIENT

It is my experience that if both client and agency enter the partnership in a collaborative way then outstanding thinking and ground-breaking communications can follow. You will know of other longstanding examples from the industry such as Levi's and BBH or VW and DDB London. What both agency and client are striving for is a platform of trust, honesty and dialogue on which to construct great communications. Here a client realizes that just because you pay for the agency's intellectual services it does not mean that you own its soul and can ultimately steer things in your direction. Conversely, an agency should not try to take either an arrogant or 'toadying position' just because it is being paid by the client.

More positively, more experienced clients have realized that by allowing a collaborative partnership to flourish they will gain a good deal more for their money: an agency partner will move from just being an expert to a trusted adviser delivering real insight, anticipating business issues and stretching a team's market thinking. Instead of ringing the agency up with a PR brief, you will want to have the agency personnel at your planning meetings for their insight. Similarly, they will come up with invaluable recommendations without needing a brief. Jagdish Sheth and Andrew Sobel discuss and explore the evolution from an 'expert for hire' to a 'trusted adviser' across a number of service sectors in *Clients for Life* (2000). Their diagram (Figure 1.7) shows where an agency ideally would like to be and ultimately where you can reap the most rewards from an agency relationship.

In *Clients for Life* (2000), Sheth and Sobel cite the transition to 'trusted advisers' as giving the following benefits:

- They add significant new perspectives to the problem or issue at hand.
- They help to focus the discussion on the most critical relevant issues.
- They provide specific ideas and solutions.
- Sometimes, clients feel their advisers are insightful when, through artful questioning, listening, and discussion, they enable clients to arrive at their own solutions.

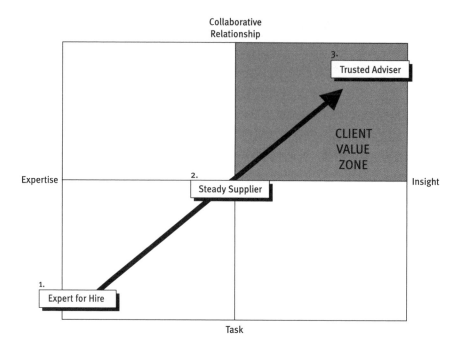

Figure 1.7   Moving into the client value zone

COMMENT

Do you have real partners?

- Do you ask your agency for advice on its specific area of expertise and on wider business issues?
- Does your agency provide real insight about customers, marketing operations, competition, etc.?
- Would you recommend your agency to others for a long-term relationship?
- Is there a strong level of trust with your agency?
- Do you believe you get value for money from your agency relationship?
- Is the agency an internal communication facilitator within your company?
- Do colleagues comment on how invaluable the agency is?
- Do you treat certain agency personnel as though they were part of your department?

A lot of agencies say that they will challenge your thinking and they do, but they 'back you against the wall' and make their challenging approach an ongoing nightmare. The better ones challenge you but help you to come to a solution with which you feel comfortable – normally because they understand your internal or business context and know how to solve the issues with you. For example, on an operational level, you brief them on a press ad and they may present a creative solution which is not a press ad – but the media equivalent of a Rubik's cube. Alternatively you have been working with the agency personnel for several years and they decide this time to throw the corporate guidelines out of the window in designing a new brochure (you can hear them saying in their black polo-necks: 'We thought this time the brief warranted revolution not evolution'). Admittedly you may not fire them on the spot as you see where they are coming from, and this may be an aberration. Yet, your boss and your sales department will not necessarily be so tolerant. If the radical nature of the concept is valid, a good agency will have prepared a creative rationale or a media argument that shows that the cube delivers the same media exposure but higher impact for the same price and/or a production cost rationale. Instead of challenging you in a 'do or die' way (you could feel they are saying 'do you have the *cojones* to present it to your sales department?') they are showing you how they will work with you every step of the way.

On an operational level, instead of telling you that you need to sack your call centre because they are 'rubbish', they may suggest working with them to help them to improve the tracking information.

Whatever it is, it should be working with you in a challenging way rather than challenging you in a bloody-minded way.

Sheth and Sobel also identify seven attributes, which contribute to a professional person/company such as an agency becoming a trusted adviser and developing a heightened collaborative relationship and adding real value:

1 **Selfless independence.** They balance loyalty to their client's agenda with an emotional independence or objectivity, which allows them to advise appropriately.
2 **Empathy.** They understand the emotions and thoughts of their clients as well as the context in which the clients operate.
3 **Conviction.** They believe strongly in what they recommend and this is motivating and energizing for both parties.
4 **Integrity.** This combination of skills and behaviours builds trust, reliability, consistency and honesty.
5 **Deep generalist.** A passion for continuous learning allows a breadth of knowledge.

6   **Synthesis.**   The ability to discern trends and patterns and see the big picture.

7   **Judgement.**   The ability to evaluate and then act in a considered way, which results in successful decisions.

TIP

If you are looking for a new agency, look out for these traits in how the agency personnel present themselves, how they work with clients (through other client endorsements) and how they work internally with each other. Ask yourself these questions related to the above attributes:

1   Are they just 'Yes people'?
2   How do they vary their approach according to the client?
3   Can you see evidence of confidence, passion and pride?
4   Do their clients trust them beyond the norm?
5   How do they think? Have they contributed strategically to any of their clients?
6   What do they think have been their best decisions?

If you inherit an agency and do not feel that its members display the right traits strongly enough, make sure you alert the agency to your concerns. One client I know called a meeting with the agency management and set out immediately how he was going to introduce new benchmarks. This prompted the agency management to change the personnel on the client's business and refresh the general way of working and in fact they managed to turn things around in three months.

STARTING OFF ON THE RIGHT FOOT

As in any type of relationship, you want to start off as you mean to go on and christen the beginning with all the goodwill possible. Whether it is a new agency or a new agency member, you have the opportunity to build a good platform for the collaborative partnership we have been discussing. It is worth noting that a new team member's introduction to your company and the agency relationship will be like anyone's first few days in a new job. The Emotion vs Induction curve in Figure 1.8 shows how you start off with initial excitement, but this will always dip into internal self-doubt. It is up to the person facilitating the induction to make sure that this rollercoaster ride of emotions is as swift as possible so that the new person becomes as effective as possible. An agency's client can do this and also extend the emotional 'honeymoon' for both client and agency by preparing a good induction programme. Any agency 'worth its salt' should be doing the same thing for you.

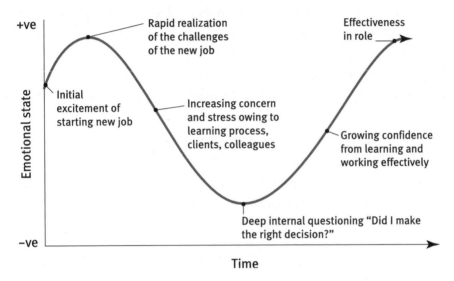

Figure 1.8   Emotional transition during initial induction

The following are a few suggestions for getting the agency personnel up to speed with your business:

- **Give them a full product induction.**   This is easier for car manufac-turers – a ride and drive event would be good but how do you do it for financial services? You could perhaps ask a product manager to give them a comprehensive product overview and make it fun with a quiz.
- **Introduce them to your research manager/agency.**   Giving them an overview of what research has been undertaken and what customer information they can tap into will be invaluable.
- **Organize visits to your retail outlets/your call centre or equivalent.** Talking to people on the 'coalface' will give them a very good insight into customer issues.

- **Ask them to present their proposals to other departments.** This will bring your colleagues into the frame and will expose the agency to the other internal players and their areas of interest.
- **Introduce them to your finance department.** This will enlighten them on the finance procedures, further any conversations and hopefully smooth a way for invoicing, etc.
- **Introduce them to your legal compliance or print departments and any other functions that will be involved in the campaign process.** If there are any functions that will be critical in developing campaigns then this may mean that both parties can assist each other rather than having an antagonistic relationship.
- **Share with them the business results and future targets.** This will make them feel essential to the business results.
- **Have each member of the core team in your office for one day.** This will help them to understand your context and give them an insight into your phone and computer systems, meetings, etc.
- **Introduce them to your other agencies.** Make sure you set the scene as to how you want them to work together.

TIP

Why not start the new agency relationship with a celebration? A new client brought a bottle of champagne to our first team kick-off meeting. On that occasion, 10.30 am was a little early for a drink but we managed to draw out the meeting to make the christening timely. It made us feel very welcome after a lengthy pitch and it did not necessarily make people think it would happen all the time. Similarly, such a gesture can lubricate an ongoing dialogue.

As much as your agency needs to get to grips with your company workings, you need to understand how the agency operates. You may wish to suggest the following to the agency:

- **You and your team sit one day in the agency.** You will also get an understanding of the context and systems, etc.
- **You spend time with the functions within the agency which will be important to you.** These could be creative, planning, data and production.

- **Understand how the agency approaches a problem.** They may have a specific methodology or personnel who deal with this. Make sure you understand your position in the process.
- **Meet the finance person.** Agencies are very keen that finances go smoothly, so this conversation will be helpful to know what their priorities are. (This could also be beneficial to your purchasing department.)

TIP

Definitely spend time with the Creative Director and ask him/her to show you some of the best work the agency has done. Understand the background and how strategic thinking added to the creative product. Also understand the results that were achieved and the emphasis that was given to these results. It will also help you to understand where your brand fits into the agency portfolio.

ENSURING THAT THE NEW TEAM WORKS WELL TOGETHER

If you are the person responsible for managing the combined agency–client team you need to make sure that the team has the right framework within which to operate. The key factors are:

- Structure.
- Protocol.
- Common goal.
- Commitment.
- Competence.
- Benchmarks of success.

Structure

You need to need to sit down with your agency contact and work out (not only in terms of agency fee) the structure of the combined team. You need to create teams on both sides who complement each other in skills and will work well together. You need to factor in equal numbers, or you may have too many agency members making demands on your team and vice-versa. You need to establish the communication lines and how this is monitored for effectiveness on both sides.

Protocol

This can range from discussing how you prefer to use the phone, voicemail and email to setting up a formal campaign processes. With timings and milestones, make sure you also determine how the team and external parties keep up to date with developments. In addition, as the client, you will need to decide how you want the agency members to communicate with your other agencies/departments. It is normally very helpful to supply an 'organogram' (reporting structure) with telephone direct lines and email addresses.

Common Goal

This seems obvious, but how many times have you really sat down as a combined internal/agency team and mapped out your mission. Is it 'to develop outstanding communications in the wider luxury sector' or 'to create marketing activity which has an excellent reputation for customer integrity'? To define how you do this, have a joint discussion, look to your brand for pointers, and canvas your managers.

Commitment

You have chosen the wrong agency if there is lack of commitment. However, you need to refresh this on a regular basis. In addition, your internal team needs to display this. A psychometric assessment can also give you a guide on how to motivate people and encourage the commitment to achieve the common goal.

Competence

Do you have the skills in the joint team to achieve your goals? For example, you may find that some of your team have never worked with agencies before.

Through formal/informal training and coaching you need to make sure that the right balance of competencies exists. If you work with your purchasing department, you may need to spend some time with them understanding what they do and showing them how you develop campaigns.

Benchmarks of Success

You should also discuss with the combined team how everybody's performance will be measured. Ask the team to make a list of the skills that are required to develop your marketing communications, then judge whether each member is adequately equipped with benchmarks of success. How will you know whether the joint team has achieved its objectives? Moreover, are there interim benchmarks that will allow you to monitor things on an ongoing basis?

TIP

You should seriously consider psychometrically assessing the team members so that everyone understands each other's styles and you can see any potential conflict issues. We all know that we have different personal working styles, but after undergoing a Myers–Briggs Type Indicator® assessment in a team, I was surprised how much empathy there was afterwards. Suddenly team members could explain things a lot better by understanding, for example, that one member approached things very analytically and this new recognition seemed to reduce the tensions.

COMMENT

How much do you know about your agency contacts? I am not suggesting that you keep CIA-like files on your team members but have a look at Figure 1.9 to gauge how much you know about them. If you understand the background to your agency contacts and their motivations, you can demonstrate empathy much better. How many of the items in Figure 1.9 could you complete?

In essence, in order to build a platform for the type of partnership that this chapter has advocated, you need to know each other well enough to have open and honest conversations. Once the heady initial honeymoon period is over,

Agency Contacts Knowledge Questionnaire

Crazy For Work
L I M I T E D

What details do you know about those you work with?

A.
Title_____ First name_____ Surname_____
Normally called_____ Nickname_____
Job title_____ Job function_____
Department_____
Address details_____
Communication means (Switchboard, Direct line, Fax, Mobile, email)_____
Home address/phone number_____

B.
Birth date and place_____
Hometown_____
Any things to remember_____
Smoker/non-smoker_____
Diet/alcohol preferences_____

C.
College/university_____
Qualifications_____
Previous agencies/companies_____

D.
Outside interests/sports_____
Marital status_____ Partner's name_____
Partner's occupation_____
Children (ages and names)_____
Car_____
Conversational interest_____

E.
How many years working at agency?_____
How many years working with your company?_____ Main contact_____
Other accounts they work on?_____
Potential to leave agency?_____

F.
Long-range business objective_____
Long-range personal objective_____
Greatest concern at present – business_____
Greatest concern at present – personal_____

Figure 1.9 Agency contacts knowledge questionnaire

you will need that basis. In addition to knowing what you want, understanding your business partners and respecting their expertise, there is a sense of trust that you will need to encourage. This will have to be earned by both sides in the day-to-day dealings but you will help it along by preparing the ground as described.

EXERCISES

1   Define your department's key skills to execute your core activity.

2   Review your induction process for agencies and newcomers to the department.

3   Complete the Agency Contacts Knowledge Questionnaire for your key contact.

HOW AN AGENCY WORKS BEHIND THE SCENES

CHAPTER 2

HOW AN AGENCY WORKS BEHIND THE SCENES

In this chapter you will learn about:

- How an agency is structured.
- The creative development process.

L ike any human relationship, a good agency–client relationship is a complex balance of personal chemistry, experience, respect and practicality. As someone involved in the relationship, you need to inspire, excite, negotiate, manage, monitor and act the diplomat. If you thought that because you were the one paying the agency for a service you would not have to do this, then I have some inevitable news for you: both sides need to act like this. You have not only to pay, but you have to play fair (well, most of the time) if you want a productive relationship. One essential requirement for that productive relationship is for both sides to understand the other party's context. As much as an agency needs to understand your company's marketplace, business issues and way of working, you will need to understand how an agency functions. This will not only help you to understand the origins of the agency's particular approach, it will give you an insight into how you can inspire it to provide you and your company with outstanding communications. In addition, if you are working with an agency that is 'best in the class', there are ways you can tap into its wider expertise and knowledge, which can benefit you even more. This chapter will provide you with a map of how your agency is structured and where you can exert the most influence.

UNDERSTANDING HOW AN AGENCY IS STRUCTURED

Every agency is different, and obviously as we could be talking about, among others, a sales promotion, PR, brand advertising, design, digital, events or a direct marketing agency, it is difficult to define the 'generic agency'. Nevertheless the book is designed for those companies who work with agencies that develop a creative product. This, therefore, is one starting point, and ultimately the final creative product is a result of strategic thinking, concept creation, creative development and production. Therefore, this also in turn gives us a framework for seeing how an agency is structured.

COMMENT

Let's go back one stage before we explore the structure in order to understand the existence of agencies: in essence, agencies sprang up as centres of specialist skill on which clients could draw to help them to develop their marketing communications. Interestingly the debate continues as to whether clients should be putting more or less into agencies to achieve more efficient integration, whether in-house resources should be exploited or whether agencies are now better equipped to offer a 'one-stop shop'. We shall return to this discussion as regards production of artwork, but it highlights that there is no 'supreme right' for agencies to exist and that agencies need to show real added value if they are to be retained.

Also, as you are the lead party in the relationship, you need to be aware of the consequences of this principal role. An agency is a client's 'agent', acting on behalf of you and your company. This is incredibly important to understand not only from a legal liability aspect but also from how you interact with the agency and its staff on a daily basis. The agency is acting on your behalf and take its lead from your direction and instructions. Consequently it is your responsibility to provide that direction and those instructions in the clearest and most effective way.

You may get swamped with contact reports, cost sign-offs and creative proposals from zealous agencies but these are all records or documents which underline the contract (virtual or tangible) that you have with your agency. No sensible agency will act without clear instructions from its client. Therefore if you expect things to happen, you will need to approve each stage and query anything with which you have issue.

TIP

When dealing with your agency, see yourself as a Premier Division football manager. You are in charge of a group of highly talented individuals who can work well as a team (Figure 2.1). You have colleagues to assist you to get the best out of your team. But you need to provide them with a game-plan to operate within, the scope to display their skills in their best way, and inspiration to excel at their game (OK, enough of the football analogy but you know what I mean).

Client Services

This function has different names in different agencies (account handling, client services, client representatives, brand team). These people are the crucial players for you. They are your representatives, champions within the agency, your ambassadors to the outside world. Make sure you have the right chemistry with these people. Could you spend a long train journey together with them? They will become your professional 'friends' (you will spend enough time with them either face-to-face or on the phone). If they are committed, they will walk through fire for you. I love the image of two of my former colleagues in the USA (Business Director and Account Director) who gave up their Sunday morning to resolve a client problem. While driving, the chief executive of a new company, which we were launching worldwide, had seen the poster advertisement on the day of the launch. In Michigan, the poster boards on highways have two sides, so the new company was sharing its exposure with a lapdancing club who had also just launched. The cardboard silhouette of the girls' arms in James Bond pose with pistols in hand extended above the poster and could be seen when you looked at the brand launch poster. Obviously the CEO was less than pleased with this brand association and made his views clear to the agency. As the poster company said that their schedule did not allow them

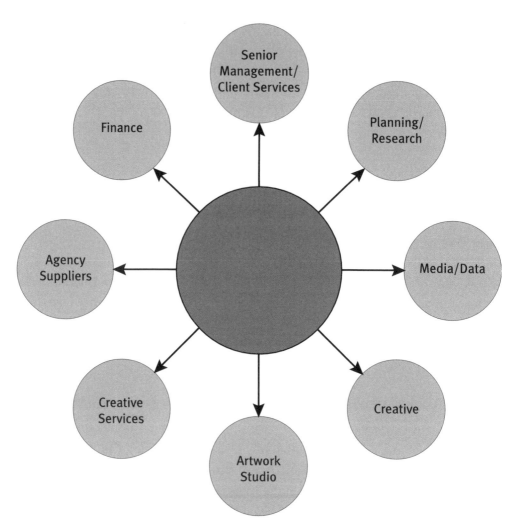

Figure 2.1   Different functions associated with an agency

to remove our poster for another two days, my US colleagues hired a 20-foot ladder and tore it off themselves! OK, it is not a daily occurrence but you sometimes need this commitment.

Account handlers are also the people who marshal and inspire all the agency forces to act on your behalf. They should be jacks of all trades and masters of them all. (OK, I admit that I may have a vested interest in these descriptions.) They are your project managers influencing timings, costs and output. They are normally the liaison with key 'executional' functions such as the creative and production departments, and in this respect they are communicating your comments and instructions to other people. They are your budget-holders and financial administrators. They are also the people who can add value in terms of strategic thinking, project efficiencies and practical suggestions at all stages of the process.

There are different levels of account handler (Graduate Trainee, Account Executive, Account Manager, Senior Account Manager/Account Supervisor, Account Director, Group Account Director, Board Director) and these titles mean different things in different agencies. (It is better to assess your account team in terms of years of experience, relevant experience, the reporting structure and identify the person who is your main daily contact, which will be a critical choice.)

What do account handlers do all day? Things always seem to take so long when you are not aware of all the stages. Figure 2.2 may help you to understand what could be a typical account handler's day (one day of a senior account manager in this case).

Time	Activity
9.00–10.00	Arrive at work and check through emails for any urgent client requests – action if required. Prepare notes for briefing studio on artwork amends on Campaign 2
10.00–10.30	Brief studio on artwork amends and agree when artwork will be available for internal approval
10.30–11.30	Attend creative briefing for Campaign 3 – running through creative brief with creative team and answering any questions. Agree date for WIP to view creative concepts
11.30–12.30	Write production brief for Campaign 4
12.30–13.00	Update Status Report for client and send to distribution list
13.00–14.00	Lunch break
14.00–15.00	Attend conference call with client to discuss new brief and agency deliverables (Campaign 5)
15.30–16.00	Revised Campaign 2 artwork from studio received – circulate for internal approval. Send to client for feedback
16.00–16.30	Reconcile costs to date for Campaign 1 – discuss with client
16.30–17.00	Update timing schedule for Campaign 4 and send to client
17.00–18.00	Start draft creative brief/proposition for new Campaign 5

Figure 2.2 A day in the life of an account handler

TIP

Once you have worked with account handlers, you should know whether they are fulfilling the above-mentioned roles on your behalf. However, at the beginning of a relationship, it is difficult to assess their potential. Maybe if deciding on a new team or team member, look for or ask about the following traits which good account handlers need to display:

- Ability to think on their feet.
- Understanding of strategic thinking and creative product.
- Organization/project management skills.
- Good communication/presentation skills.
- Enthusiasm, commitment and passion.
- Desire to work as a team player.
- Ability to manage your expectations.
- Good understanding of human nature/people skills.
- Ability to juggle and be flexible.
- Diplomatic/ambassadorial skills with third parties.
- Ability to keep a cool head.
- Attention to detail.
- Relentless intellectual curiosity about your business, your customers, your competitors.

This is not an exhaustive list but, in determining with the senior management of the agency who should work on your business, look for real evidence of those attributes. Everyone will say that they are passionate, organized, really interested in your business, but dig deeper – look for (1) examples of this, (2) previous client references, (3) colleagues' descriptions, etc. (Ask the client services director for them.) Also they may have all those qualities but they may not have the sense of humour, a 'down–to–earthness', etc., you require for the culture of your company. In other words, are they right for the task, right for you and right for your brand?

COMMENT

There are some agencies that may have client-facing functions but do not have account handlers in name. The agency Mother prides itself on having *Strategists* and *Mothers*. Digital agencies may just have *Project Managers*. Smaller agencies may have senior players in the style of Renaissance 'actor/director/managers' who fulfil many roles. Whatever the structure, you will be liaising with someone who, even if he/she is not called an account handler, will need these skills. So do something that is often assumed to be 'not possible': make sure you have some say in their choice as you will be working with them very closely.

Senior Management

These people may or may not be the owners of the agency. What unites them all is a financial interest in the success of the business and an awareness that you, as a client, contribute to that success. It really depends on the nature and size of their business whether they are involved in your account.

At the outset of the relationship, understanding the senior management gives you an indication of a number of things. As figureheads of the agency, they will give an insight into the culture of the agency. If you understand their vision for the agency, you will know where your company's account stands in realizing/adding to that vision. For example, if you are a low-income, niche luxury brand, you may not be seen as a primary income account but they may see you as essential for enhancing the agency's creative reputation. If you are a high-income account, you will start to understand your influence on their business and vice versa. (*NB*: You must ask yourself whether you want to have the agency dependent on your account as this has advantages and disadvantages, the latter including a moral dilemma of a number of people's livelihoods linked to your business.) Also if their primary activity is PR and you want them to do sales promotion in addition to PR, you should ask yourself whether the vision and resources of the agency could cope with this diversity.

Senior management, whether they were originally account handlers, creative or planners, may play an active role in your business. Do you want this (in terms of how much it will cost)? Do you require this (in terms of added strategic and creative thinking)? Do you think it is realistic to expect them to be active on your business? Some companies complain of senior management exiting stage-left after the pitch, only to be seen at the Christmas Lunch. How will it work with the rest of the agency team? Is this the most efficient way to operate?

The personalities of the senior management will also give you an indication of the style and characteristics of the people they employ to work with you.

COMMENT

Senior agency management are often very useful in raising issues outside the day-to-day practices. Sometimes it can also be invaluable to have a senior agency figure talking to your company management, bringing up issues that you know you would not be able to raise alone.

Account Planning

Stanley Pollitt, one of the founders of the agency BMP (now DDB London), is credited with developing the role of modern account planning in London of the late 1960s. The role of a planner is to champion and represent the viewpoint of the customers within the framework of the communications strategy. For example, it is very easy to lose sight of what the customers really think and how they could react by getting sucked into the product team's enthusiasm for their new launch. The planner provides a more objective and analytical way of developing communications around the customers' needs, perceptions and context. They ultimately develop customer insights which feed into the communications proposition (see Chapter 4). Planners use and commission research to develop the required customer understanding. They liaise with the account team and client to formulate the strategy, write the creative briefs and develop measurement mechanisms. You will notice that good planners display certain characteristics:

- Objectivity.
- Analytical skills.
- Data literacy.
- Creative literacy.
- Curiosity in people and your business.
- Practicality.
- Communication skills.
- Certain project management skills (to run research, etc.).

Jon Steel in *Truth, Lies and Advertising: The Art of Account Planning* (1998) reckons that there is always a little weird streak to planners to help them to see things differently. He quotes a planning colleague who heard that Jon was scared of travelling on planes because of bomb threats. He asked if Jon had considered taking his own bomb with him as he theorized that the chances of two separate bombs on the same plane had to be miniscule. It is a delightful example of the lateral thinking that could come in useful in communications planning. So do not just look upon them as account handlers with bigger brains. They see the world in a different way.

Once again, the 'long train journey test' is pertinent as you may easily be travelling all over the country with them to view focus groups together. It is no exaggeration that certain planners could attend over 60 groups in one year.

COMMENT

There are certain agencies that place great store on planning. Others do not have planners. In certain brand advertising agencies, planners are the key individuals while the junior account handlers are the stereotypical 'bag carriers'. Certain direct marketing agencies say their senior management fulfil the role of planners. Whatever the set-up between account handlers and planners in your agency, make sure you have the right balance of the analytical objectivity which the planner provides and the proactive practical thinking an account handler should also give. This is important as you will sometimes get political expediency from account handlers when in fact you need the harsh truth from planners to strengthen your campaign.

The Creative Team

A 'traditional' creative team is made up of a copywriter and an art director. However, design agencies and digital agencies may vary in this respect by having designers working in isolation or with visualizers, programmers or Mac operators. A creative team should be able to receive a conventionally constructed brief and see it from a totally innovative angle. Their curiosity about the world and how people can view things should inform their ability to develop a campaign theme or big idea which will connect with customers and force them to re-evaluate their existing behaviour. There are two major stages: *concept development* and *concept execution*.

In the first stage of the creative process the division of skills is irrelevant. In creating concepts, the team concentrates on the campaign idea, therefore the art director may come up with the headline thought and the copywriter may come up with a series of images. It is only when a concept is approved that their individual crafting skills of art direction and copywriting come into play.

The creative director is normally head of the creative department and is the embodiment of the creative philosophy of the agency. He/she is responsible for overall creative quality control and may or may not work on actual campaigns.

COMMENT

Some agency clients feel intimidated by creative teams. There are apocryphal stories of heated arguments breaking out, clients being grabbed by their throats (surely agency myths to ward off over-zealous clients' criticisms?) and clients rewriting ads in front of the copywriter (surely a client myth to encourage copywriters to take on board their comments?). I think it is worth remembering that some creative teams are very comfortable and experienced in working with clients face-to-face. However, there are some who feel very unsure and inexperienced in articulating their ideas to external parties. The best teams are those who can feed into a productive and creative discussion with you, while remaining true to the big idea and the customer viewpoint. Moreover, there is a new school of agencies in which the creative teams actively engage with clients and welcome the dialogue in order to prevent later disappointment. I believe this is a much better way of working, and a client who spends time to understand the creative mentality will reap the rewards in the work. I noticed an example of this a few years ago when a client was getting on famously with a particular creative head. It turned out he had decided to get actively involved in judging panels and creative debates and now he had a stronger bond to those who had been with him at such events. It also influenced how he saw our conceptual work and how the teams engaged with him in the creative development process. I think both sides genuinely benefited.

Media/Data

There are obviously specialist agencies who deal with media and data. When I talk about media and data planning, I am describing the planning function within agencies (traditionally, media in brand advertising agencies and data in direct marketing agencies). A media planner is someone who will have an understanding of the public media through which your marketing messages can be channelled to reach your customers at the most cost-effective price. Using the budget available, they will then draw up a media plan to optimize exposure, frequency and impact of the message to your customers.

A data planner will be doing a very similar job, but formulating a plan which identifies how to reach the target group directly by using your marketing databases and/or external lists. He/she may use profiling, segmentation and modelling techniques to refine his/her knowledge or targeting.

Both planners will need a good understanding from you of the appeal of your product/service and your communications objectives. They should display similar characteristics to account planners but they also need to have analytical tools at their disposal to construct hypothetical success models (i.e. testing strategies) and dissect results to understand marketing effectiveness.

Historically, there have been the stereotypes of the media person with the wide banter and the penchant for long lunches, and the data planner with the pointy head and the incomprehensible charts, but I think a lot of that is changing as client and agency personnel become more sophisticated and these planners become more integral to the agency offering.

TIP

Certain agencies/account handlers do not involve media or data planners at an early enough stage. This may be because of internal divisions or politics between agencies. As they are critical to the planning of a communications campaign, ensure that you have direct contact with these functions to maintain their involvement throughout the process. I cannot imagine that if Naked had not been involved at the launch planning of the 118 118 directory enquiry service, it would have been such a success – think of those placements in barber shops and charity shops on the high street and those moustachioed runners cropping up everywhere.

Creative Services

1   Traffic.
2   Art buying.
3   Production.

The role of traffic is to ensure the smooth flow of creative work so that deadlines are met – literally moving the work through the agency, making sure that any issues are discussed and acquiring quality control approvals. Art buyers preside over the purchase and use of illustrations and film/photography. The production function (whether the work is print, digital or film) oversees the stage of creative development which is ultimately going to be seen or experienced by the customers. These roles can be embodied by one person or split accordingly.

TIP

In these days of tighter deadlines and diversified roles you need to make sure of the following:

- Determine whether you or the agency is responsible for the tasks of art buying and production.
- Clearly state what role you wish to play in the various stages (sign-offs, quality control checks and photographic shoots).
- Make sure the development process is transparent to you.
- Understand the milestones and agree the quality checks.
- Have sight of/approve the various production briefs (TV, photography, print specs, mailing/lasering/data selections, photography usage, etc.).
- Provide any guidelines where necessary.

Artwork Studio/Digital Production

You will tend not to deal with the studio or digital production directly. Yet I can guarantee you that this is an area where there will be friction between you and the agency. As the deadline looms, this is where delivery becomes critical and cost is an important factor. As a number of marketers also have studio and web programming in-house, it throws up a few issues on who does what, how quickly and how much it will cost.

At the outset of a campaign you obviously need to decide with the agency who is going to fulfil these functions – though it is not always a black and white decision. For example, your in-house artwork studio may be cheaper because it is subsidized by the overall company structure but you, as a campaign manager, then become the liaison with the studio. You act as account handler and quality control checker – which will draw on your time. On the agency side, they are often keen to retain the artwork in order to ensure a consistent development of the creative concept which can have a positive effect for you; it means that you as a client are shielded from some of the extraneous development issues.

So how do you decide if you have an in-house studio and the flexibility to use either? I would suggest the following: standardize costs, timings and procedures between the agency's studio and the company's studio. Trial the route that works best for you and then decide. If you cannot standardize the processes and costs, trial both routes and monitor them closely for efficiency.

Finance

You may not deal directly with the finance function of the agency. On the agency side there may be an accountant, a finance director or a whole department looking after (i) invoicing and aged debt, (ii) supplier payment and (iii) income and profitability.

A good agency will give a lot of weight to this function. Ultimately an agency only has its time to sell and it needs to recoup its staff's time in a financially effective way. This will be looked at in more detail in Chapter 7 but with a number of agencies historically mismanaging this side of the business you will now find that the finance department is staffed with people who are well qualified to ensure financial stability and maintain rigour in this area.

UNDERSTANDING THE CREATIVE DEVELOPMENT PROCESS

The agency will be experienced in developing and implementing creative campaigns. As a number of milestones and gateways are critical to a campaign's progress, it is up to you and the agency to agree how these stages are reached and what approval processes and quality control checks are to be in place. This is essential for a new client–agency team and may take some time to evolve into the most efficient way of working. The key stages are shown in Figure 2.3.

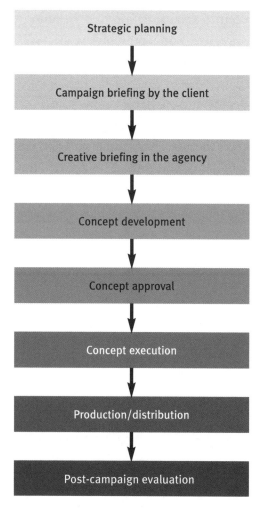

Figure 2.3 Stages in campaign development process

Strategic Planning

If there is one stage to get right more than any other, this is it. Potentially this is your greatest leverage point, the stage where you can exert the greatest influence to be transmitted along the line all the way to the marketplace. This is where you look at the business objective, understand the marketplace and customer issues and subsequently formulate the communications strategy and the indicators of success. This checklist may help you to make sure that you cover all the areas to be explored:

1 Is the business objective quantified (e.g. in terms of sales, timing, etc.)?
2 Is the business objective realistic (or does it need to be refined)?
3 What are your previous campaign learnings?
4 What is the real competitive set (do you need to think more broadly as to who the competition is)?
5 Do you have a good analysis of your product/service versus the competition?
6 What is the desired product/service positioning?
7 What is the company brand positioning and how does the product positioning leverage the brand?
8 Do you have real customer insight about the product/service? Is the best research available or do you need to commission specific research?
9 What will be the benchmarks of success (and how will they be practically measured)?
10 Can the internal systems/resources support such a campaign?
11 Do you have the right people in the planning sessions?

TIP

Potentially, the first planning meeting can be a nebulous event as everyone's thinking is obviously quite embryonic. At the same time this initial meeting should set the tone for an inspiring campaign. For major campaigns, you may want to think about involving the agency at this stage. They are normally well qualified to facilitate a brainstorm and they not only feel involved in the inception but they also provide an 'external' viewpoint. You may, however, decide that there should first be an internal meeting and involve the agency at the second half of the planning stage.

Campaign and Creative Briefings

These areas are explored in depth in Chapter 4. Once you have a good grasp of the objectives/strategy and market/customer issues you will need to issue a campaign brief. This is a clear set of instructions which determine what you require from the agency in terms of developing creative work. The agency in turn develops a creative brief. This is a refinement of the thinking in your brief and is addressed specifically to the creative team. At this stage you may also be issuing other briefs such as to your media agency, internal contact centre and your internal communications department.

Concept Development

Once the briefs have been approved, the creative team can start to think about developing a concept. This is the pure idea or theme that is derived from the brief's single-minded proposition.

Before the agency personnel present their ideas to you, it is worth confirming what you are expecting and what they are going to deliver. This discussion needs to relate to what level of finish it is going to be (simple black and white drawings or Mac-generated visuals – see Figure 2.4). In addition, some agencies present 'adcepts' which can look like posters or press ads (just an image and a headline) and once the idea has been approved they then work out the practicalities for individual media.

The level of finish and 'media readiness' depends on the time, cost and your or your colleagues' level of comfort with simple drawings.

Concept Execution

Once the concept is approved (discussed in more detail in Chapter 6), the copywriter and art director take their specialist areas and develop them further.

Source: Reproduced by permission of Partners Andrews Aldridge and Lexus GB, 2004. Actual format 4pp.

Figure 2.4   Examples of a black and white visual and a Mac visual. Two press insert concepts based on the same proposition

Within the agency, there will probably be a pre-production meeting to anticipate the need for new photography, a director, events coordinator, etc., depending on the media route. As a result of this meeting an accurate cost estimate and timing schedule should be issued to you for your approval.

When it comes to this point with print materials, it is also worth requesting a Mac visual layout (particularly if what has been presented has been a black and white drawing) to show you how the type and images will roughly be laid out.

Production/Distribution

Chapter 6 deals with the project management aspect of this area. However the book will not go into the real detail of production as this depends on the medium through which the creative idea is being communicated. Broadcast, digital and print all have their own peculiarities so you need to make sure that the agency is qualified in this area and keeps you informed throughout the process.

EXERCISES

1   Name the qualities your account team displays in your day-to-day encounters.

2   Assess whether you have the right level of account planning on your business.

3   Map out and review the normal campaign process with the agency.

SELECTING AN AGENCY

CHAPTER 3

SELECTING AN AGENCY

In this chapter you will learn about:

- Preparation before an agency review.
- Working with third-party specialists.
- Guidelines on agency search and selection.
- Meeting the agency face-to-face.
- Post-pitch feedback.

Those who have sat in an agency pitch presentation and sadly realized within 10 minutes that they are not going to hear what they were hoping for know the value of preparing the groundwork when selecting an agency. It is an area as familiar to many as it is foreign to others. It is estimated by AAR that in the UK approximately 750 companies review their agency line-up each year (including media arrangements) and (re-)allocate a total marketing budget of £2.2 billion. Whether you are new to the process or a pitch veteran, if you decide to review your agency arrangements there is no avoiding the consequences – you are in for endless meetings, introductions and PowerPoint® slides. And at times you will wonder whether there is a better way of finding a new agency. There are a few new developments and understandably the process has been streamlined, but if you invite this type of courtship you will find that you have a plethora of suitors ready with their equivalent of flowers and love letters. But all is not doom and gloom: in the time you spend hunting down your new agency partner you have the invaluable opportunity of seeing your business issues (and even colleagues) in a different light, meeting some of the smartest, most inspirational people in the business and being exposed to radically new ways of reaching your customers.

So if this is virgin territory to you, how do you go about understanding the agency landscape and finding that new partner? Fortunately, this is an area in which a number of trade bodies and third-party consultants can provide assistance. Any marketers who set off on a course of potentially changing their agency will be glad of such help as it can be a time-consuming and sometimes stressful activity. In this chapter I shall be using the joint industry guidelines (developed by the IPA, ISBA, MCCA, DMA and PRCA) as a framework for considering and implementing an agency review. The guidelines are accessible from each of the trade bodies' websites. I shall also be adding further commentary to illustrate the day-to-day practicalities of the whole process.

COMMENT

There are a number of reasons why you may want to select a new agency – this could be your first time, you could be dissatisfied with your existing arrangement, you could be considering the launch of a new brand or accommodating a conflict of business.

There are different ways to find the right agency but first of all it may be worth looking at a conventional sequence of events in the process to understand the subsequent sections. Although there are interim steps and variations that will be discussed later, these could be the various milestones for a particular client:

1   Recognition that an existing agency relationship is not tenable.
2   Identifying potential suitable agencies.
3   Creation of a 'longlist' of agencies to get to know.
4   Introductory or 'chemistry' meetings.
5   Determining the shortlist of agencies.
6   Briefing of the shortlisted agencies.

7   Final agency presentations.
8   Final selection of agency.
9   Announcement and handover.

PREPARATION BEFORE AN AGENCY REVIEW

Planning an agency review in advance not only makes you use your and your colleagues' time efficiently, it also makes you think about the consequences your decision will have for your company, your existing agency and the candidate agencies you enlist. It helps you to set the scope of the selection process and allows you to understand what internal and external help you will need. The joint industry guidelines are invaluable in this area:

Ten Key Considerations before Undertaking a Review

The selection and retention of the right agency is critical for a client because of the key role that your communications agencies are able to play in promoting your company and its brands, thus enhancing your ultimate profitability. Long-term relationships benefit the health of brands. Therefore the following key points should be considered before embarking on an agency search:

1   **Why are you reviewing?**   Be very clear that changing the agency would be in the best interests of the brand or the business organization, and will enhance shareholder value. Before embarking on a search for a new agency, be really sure that best efforts have been made to restore the existing client–agency relationship to health. Consider using third-party consultants to facilitate this process.

2   **Do you have full buy-in?**   If a review is deemed to be the right course of action, ensure that the client company's top management fully endorse it, and that the key decision-makers are clearly identified and enlisted in the process.

3   **Is purchasing involved?**   If your company has a purchasing function, then marketing or corporate communications should involve these colleagues from the outset, to ensure value is added overall, rather than just bringing them in at the end to discuss the contract and terms.

4   **Should you get outside help?**   It is now quite normal for client companies to seek outside professional help from both the trade bodies and the specialist intermediaries. We would certainly recommend that you do, and they have all contributed to *Finding an Agency*. You will find that they can give you step-by-step guidance during the search and selection process.

5   **Have you checked the contracts?**   Before the process begins you should check the provisions within your contract with your incumbent agency, particularly with regard to the notice period and termination of contract.

6   **How will you inform your current agency?**   You should consider the implications of informing your existing agency that the review of arrangements is taking place, weighing the need for confidentiality against the scenario of the incumbent finding out about the review from a source other than their client.

7   **Do you have a clear brief?**   Gain full agreement with all those involved in the decision-making process about the requirements of the agency. Invest time and effort in agreeing the budget and producing a written brief describing the brand or company's current position and future requirements in the context of clear marketing and business objectives. Decide whether the client is acting as the orchestrator of a series of agency relationships, needs a 'lead' agency, or requires a 'one-stop-shop'.

8   **What kind of pitch will you hold?**   Give some thought to the type of pitch that will best assist you in making the appointment; the traditional pitch process is expensive for both parties, so agree fees where appropriate to offset a fair proportion of the agency costs and to assure a professional approach on both sides. Note that many successful agency appointments are based on reputation, personal chemistry, credentials and references from other clients, as opposed to pitches. Workshops and trial projects are also effective methods of choosing an agency.

9   **Do you require confidentiality?**   Before the search process begins, you and the participating agencies both need to consider entering into a mutual confidentiality/non-disclosure agreement to deal with issues concerning copyright and intellectual property. This should cover materials supplied by you for the pitch, and those produced by the agency in response.

10   **How will you handle publicity?**   It is advisable to prepare a communications strategy about the agency review in advance, including a press release, so that you are prepared to deal with approaches from the trade press if news of the pitch is leaked at any stage during the process.

Source: Finding an Agency – Joint industry guidelines reproduced by permission of DMA, IPA, ISBA, MCCA and the PRCA (2004). Fully downloadable from each of the trade bodies' websites (addresses in the Useful Information Sources section).

'Why are you reviewing?' has to be the first question. The second question in that vein is 'Is there no alternative?'. If you go to any specialist, they will handle you a bit like a divorce lawyer does – they want your business but they are morally bound to tell you that it can be messy, costly and not always the best thing for the short term. Of course, you will be courted by a number of agencies who all will be vying for your business but do not underestimate the time you and your team will have to invest in the stages additional to those mentioned in the previous comment section:

- Achieving internal approval for a pitch.
- Deciding on the trade body/third-party specialist to work with in the pitch process.
- Briefing the trade body/third-party.
- Sifting through the longlist information provided (see Figure 3.1).
- Providing internal access or sufficient information to the agencies.
- Conducting the agency presentation debrief.
- Handling the journalists' enquiries and subsequent publicity.
- Handling unsolicited agency enquiries.
- Managing transition campaigns between the incumbent and new agency.
- Bringing the new agency up to speed with you, your team, your business, your partner departments, your other agencies, etc.

AAR estimates that holding a pitch can cost a client around £50 000 in terms of time and resource and this does not take into account the disruption to the brand that could follow. Therefore you should not initiate a pitch to shake up an existing agency relationship which is redeemable. You may have noticed that the chocolate biscuits have been replaced by ginger ones at agency meetings and are wondering who is now getting the executive treatment. Yet if you feel that the human relationship aspect has not broken down, it may be that you can rescue the other aspects by bringing your concerns to the notice of the agency management.

After consideration, your decision may not be to hold a review process as the short-term damage to the brand and the associated costs may be prohibitive. It may be best to work the issues through with your incumbent agency. You may also decide you wish to elicit the help of an industry 'marriage counsellor' (see comment below on getting outside help). Try constructing a decision matrix such as the one in Figure 3.2 to help you to assess what the important criteria are in the existing relationship and whether the issues are resolvable. Such a matrix allows you to take some of the emotion and subjectivity out of the issues with the agency and curtail the potentially premature desire to reach for the phone and get a new agency in.

AGENCY LONGLIST QUESTIONNAIRE

1. Company location

Provide agency's name, address, internet url, telephone, fax and key numbers. List all other UK offices/addresses. Describe the agency's ownership or any affiliations with networks or trading arrangements with other companies.

2. Agency personnel

List the senior management team and include their summary C.V.s. Provide brief biographies of key management executives in each department. Include the name, title, e-mail address and mobile phone number of the individual who will serve as agency's primary client contact during the pitch process.

3. Clients

List the agency's top 10 clients indicating each client's tenure with agency.
List accounts won over the past two years and the date appointed.
List accounts lost or resigned over the past two years.
Provide testimonial letters and named referees from amongst the agency's current clients.

4. Financial

Describe the agency's ownership structure.
Provide a copy of the agency's latest report and accounts as lodged at Companies House.
Summarise billings and income for the past two years, including a forecast for the current year. In the case of start-ups, or very new agencies, clients may ask to see the agency business plan and understand the financial support they have.
Segment clients anonymously according to billing and position the prospective client in context.
Provide percentage breakdown of the responding office's billings by media type or discipline covered (eg TV, radio, magazines, newspapers, outdoor, direct, interactive, etc.).

5. Remuneration

Describe the agency policy with respect to method of remuneration i.e. fee, commission, minimum income guarantee, payment by results (PBR), royalties or other/combination.
Submit a draft agency contract.

6. Strategic approach

Describe the processes and methods which the agency employs to develop effective marketing communications for brands.
Describe how the agency evaluates the effectiveness of its work for clients.

7. Services

Summarise briefly the range of marketing communications services the agency offers clients, indicating particular strengths.

8. Relevant experience

Describe agency's relevant experience.
Provide at least two case histories dealing with similar or analogous issues.
In no more than two pages, describe why agency is ideally suited to address the challenges and opportunities of the account in question, as set out in the client brief.

9. Awards

List the creative and effectiveness awards the agency has won over the past three years, if relevant to the discipline or project.

10. Creative work

Provide samples of your creative work, with brief rationales and evidence of effectiveness.

Source: Finding an Agency – Joint industry guidelines reproduced by permission of DMA, IPA, ISBA, MCCA and the PRCA (2004). Fully downloadable from each of the trade bodies' websites (addresses in the Useful Information Sources section).

Figure 3.1   Agency longlist questionnaire

Relationship aspect	Evaluation	Issue	Fixability?	Action
Knowledge of business	3	Senior agency players unaware of business issues.	5	Involve agency management in internal meetings, trade shows etc.
Pan-European support	4	n/a	n/a	n/a
Strategic input	3–4	Sporadic input.	4	Get agency working with lead agency.
Creative product	2	Uninspiring. Too long a process.	3	Talk to agency. Regular creative reviews.
Campaign implementation	4	n/a	n/a	n/a

(Scoring 1–5: 1 = very low, 5 = very high)

Figure 3.2   Relationship fixability matrix

COMMENT

Particularly if you were responsible for appointing the incumbent agency, you will feel potentially implicated in their failure to deliver. You may feel that internally it is a reflection on your reputation. Unfortunately these things happen and if you believe that you have done everything to assist them, you will know you will have to take steps to make sure that your company is being served well. Once you have taken a more detached position and detailed where the agency is falling down and established that it is not retrievable, you need to communicate this to your boss and team and any relevant departments, such as purchasing and agency/supplier management. I would suggest that you involve them to make a collaborative decision about looking for a new agency and then this will bind them into the various stages of the selection process. Purchasing can also be useful at an early stage as they will flag up any contractual issues when exiting from the existing relationship.

TIP

Before you start the selection process, write down what you are looking for in an agency. Going back to the divorce and romantic relationship analogy, we all may want a Cameron Diaz look-a-like with a certificate in Porsche maintenance and an uncanny knack in automatically alphabetizing our music collection or a Brad Pitt type with the ability to multitask and a disdain for sport and the TV remote control. Yet are we realistically going to find this? Also, be careful as it is easy to be 'on the rebound' from an agency relationship, looking for all the opposite characteristics of the incumbent agency. When you are looking for a new recruit to your team, you put together a recruitment brief. Why not formulate what you are looking for in a similar way? See Figure 3.3.

WORKING WITH THIRD-PARTY SPECIALISTS

You will need to decide whether you want to work with a third-party company specializing in helping you to find a new agency. My suggestion is that you should definitely do this (1) if your team is new to this process (they can help to guide you through the different stages) and/or (2) if you want them to act as a filter between you and the agency (which means that your time is used more efficiently).

The main companies who are known for their assistance in the search, selection, auditing, benchmarking and counselling of agency relationships across the major agency disciplines are:

The AAR Group	www.aargroup.co.uk
Agency Assessments International	www.agencyassessments.com
Agency Insight	www.agencyinsight.com
Creative Brief	www.creativebrief.com
The Haystack Group	www.thehaystackgroup.com

TIP

Half of the content in the marketing press relates to the changeover of agencies and rumours that surround this. Clients comment on how they are amazed how news of a pitch gets into the press. You should realize that rumours of pitches are common currency between marketing journalists and new business contacts at agencies. It may not necessarily be leaked by the agencies you are dealing with but such news always gets around. It may be through an agency that has not been successful at a particular stage. So be prepared and try to put certain mechanisms in place which can reduce the chance of public exposure. Also, do not be put off by the 'loose tongues' experience you may encounter at this juncture. Existing business in an agency does not have the same dynamic, and an agency can be trusted to maintain ongoing commercial confidentialities.

Initial Agency Requirement

Crazy For Work
L I M I T E D

Purpose of Relationship with Agency

To deliver strategic thinking and creative campaigns, leading to the marketing department acquiring and retaining customers in a profitable way.

Roles and Relationships

- To enhance our understanding of the relationship between consumers and our brand
- To deliver an impactful creative approach
- To develop strategic communication plans
- To assist in the development and use of our membership database
- To implement the creative campaigns so that they reach the marketplace effectively and efficiently
- To be jointly accountable for market success

Skill Set Required

- Consumer brand planning skills
- Superior creative expertise in our sector
- Experience in data modelling and analysis
- Familiarity with media such as press, posters, direct mail, events and web
- In-house production department
- Excellent project management skills
- Excellent liaison skills

Budget: €1.5 m

Traits/Characteristics

- Small to medium-sized agency in Edinburgh
- Award-winning creative
- Lack of preciousness/pretentiousness
- Down to earth nature of account handling
- Practical planning

What type of agency would you call this?

☐ Brand Advertising	☐ Digital Marketing	☑ Integrated
☐ PR	☐ Direct Marketing	
☐ Sales Promotion	☐ Event Management	

Figure 3.3   Initial agency requirement considerations

The following may help you in your quest for a 'low profile' while you are looking for a new agency:

- Be prepared (even if you wish to keep it out of the press) that your search could end up as a story.
- Agree a press release or internal line if the press get hold of the story.
- Tell your incumbent agency that you are considering a review (the marketing community is so small it will get back to them even if you do not tell them).
- Ask the agencies to sign a confidentiality agreement.
- Hold initial meetings at the agencies rather than at your HQ. (If you want to keep things 'under wraps', do not sign the visitors' book and ask not be kept waiting in reception.)

GUIDELINES ON AGENCY SEARCH AND SELECTION

There are different ways to assess an agency's potential contribution to your business. What you are assessing is their suitability essentially through their reputation, relevant experience, references, personal chemistry and their response to your brief. Here are the main variations of ways in which it has been done in the past once a longlist of agencies has been determined:

1 Written brief from the client. No client/agency interaction. Written strategic response/video with 'housekeeping' questions answered. Agency is chosen.

2 Written brief from the client (no initial interaction for the longlist stage). Strategic response is forwarded by the agency. Final listing presentation. Agency is chosen.

3 Face-to-face 'chemistry' meetings are held to create a shortlist. Creative and strategic presentations from the shortlist. Agency is chosen.

4 At shortlist stage, workshop is used to tackle a brief in a 'live' situation. Agency is chosen.

5 At shortlist stage, one agency is given a trial project. Agency is chosen or not.

6 A shortlist of agencies is given a trial project. One agency is chosen.

The relatively recent developments in the evolution of the selection process are the use of (1) workshops, (2) trial projects and (3) assisted pitches. They are finding popularity as people strive to create more realistic circumstances.

Workshops throw the candidates into an environment in which a brief is worked on and the performance in the live situation is assessed accordingly. It tends to be longer than a traditional pitch, may be all day and is often video-recorded. What clients find good about this process is that they can evaluate agencies under pressure and can see how the team works together and prioritizes, and how the output is derived. In addition, the 'Big Brother TV' effect can be increased by seeing how the agency works with other parties. This can be with other incumbent agencies to judge how integration can be achieved through the combined fit of the different agencies. Alternatively, it can be with the client team and other internal departments. Or the workshop can be held with all the competing agencies participating – which is interesting for the selectors as you get the intense heat of rivalry at times but which certain agencies do not like because they feel that they are in a 'show dogs' beauty parade.

This can work to your advantage in terms of time as although it is demanding on the actual day, you will not need to give the agencies so much preparation time as a normal pitch (maybe a week in contrast to 4–6 weeks for a normal pitch). This might be important if your timeframes of working with an agency and having activity in the marketplace are tight.

Whichever format you consider, remember that you will need an experienced third-party company to facilitate this and that it is best to understand the specific workshop protocol in advance to know whether you and your colleagues will be comfortable evaluating in this environment.

The *trial project* allows you to limit your risk of selecting another agency and does not mean that you have to terminate the relationship with your incumbent agency. I think the trial project works best when you have a roster of agencies. Consequently, as your incumbent agencies hear that you are testing a new agency, you can justify it by highlighting your preference for having a roster of agencies and using different agencies for their different strengths. However, having a roster is not an essential prerequisite (though it may lead you to creating a roster) but you will need to work out how you position this with your incumbent. What it gives you is a trial platform to work with a new agency on a real live brief from planning to implementation, as opposed to seeing in a classic pitch the outcome of an artificial brief only up to concept stage. You work with the real team and encounter real issues together, which allows you to evaluate their performance more realistically. I think you should also consider that you need to build in a realistic allocation of extra resource and time as you will be working with a company for the first time (as well as working with the incumbent). Also you need to choose a project that allows the best evaluation (selecting the project that has stumped your last two agencies may identify the new agency as 'head and shoulders above the rest' but it very well may stump them and not give you a good indication of their worth). Finally, you should also weigh up the confidentiality aspect. If you are working on a live project with a new agency, they will be exposed to business-sensitive information.

Something which is also gaining current momentum is what I refer to as an *'assisted pitch'*: the brief is issued, the agency involves the client at creative 'work in progress' stage and the client, being in a position of greater knowledge and experience, then shares their thoughts to make the campaign more appropriate to the brand and the challenge in hand. This technique has been employed unofficially in the past when an agency has a friendly contact at the client company and shows work in advance, but the basis of an 'assisted pitch' is a 'level playing field' so all agencies get this interim feedback and assistance. I would say that the success of this method depends on the strength of the individual campaign ideas and the decision-making hierarchy. The agencies need to come up with equally strong ideas or the final presentation will be a *fait accompli*. And unless the whole decision-making team sits in on the review processes, an individual may steer the agency in a direction that is not representative of the final combined team's view. This last point therefore means that it can be quite time-consuming because an extra stage is added. Nevertheless the agency is not working in such a vacuum and the client gets more exposure to the agency and their thinking. Moreover, if the work is to be used, then this stage is essential.

COMMENT

There needs to be responsibility on both sides in this whole process. I was involved in a pitch where, after time had been spent on answering the brief and shooting a video on the client's request (as there was no face-to-face meeting), it transpired that we were one of 20 agencies to be invited to execute this select task. Not only do I see that as very low odds for an agency to win (and a very speculative investment considering that, on average in the UK, agencies invest £20 000 plus personnel time on each pitch) but how could the client process so many tenders and decide between the offerings?

There was also a recent incident where one agency definitely spent more than the average on pitching to a well-known brand, won it and then was told that the local client had not had approval from the international HQ in the USA who was also conducting its own pitch – on a global basis! Unfortunately the UK agency lost out on the global realignment and was never officially appointed.

Conversely, an agency should be sensible enough to decide that it cannot handle a number of pitches at the same time or run a pitch when there are labour-intensive existing client projects going through the agency. The recent story in the press of a badly handled pitch is not the first time that a client has felt as though the agency is fielding the 'C team'.

In all three cases, the stories were circulated around the grapevine and I know it has not done any of the brands any good in this regard.

At this point it is worth looking further at the joint industry guidelines. The objective of the 10-stage search process outlined below is to optimize the quality of agency response and the likelihood of selecting the ideal, long-term partner. The principles apply to the appointment of any type of communications agency.

1   Prepare all the necessary background information

- Prepare an outline brief, including a clear indication of the brand or company marketing/communications budget.
- Consider the type of agency required, e.g. in terms of size relative to budget, location and specialization, potentially conflicting business, etc., and carefully draw up the criteria that will form your checklist against which to judge the initial agency list.
- Approach trade bodies such as the DMA, IPA, ISBA, MCCA and PRCA for guidance and advice if appropriate. Evaluate the importance of agency accreditation by a trade body. Members of PRCA, for example, all hold its independently audited Consultancy Management Standard.
- Identify relevant existing work for other clients, within the appropriate communications discipline, which you rate highly.
- Talk to colleagues in other companies about their agency experiences.

- Undertake any necessary desk research, consulting agency directories, trade associations and the trade press for additional background information about agencies that might interest you. Employ a consultant if you lack detailed knowledge of agencies.
- Seek credentials information from, and possibly talk with, selected agencies that match the criteria in your outline brief. Be aware, however, of the dangers of information on your search becoming widely known. Early, uncontrolled leaks can lead to you being inundated with unsolicited approaches from agencies, can damage your relationship with your incumbent if they are not aware of your plans, and can reduce your overall control of the project.
- Consider other professional, objective and confidential sources of information and assistance (lists available from the DMA, IPA, ISBA, MCCA and PRCA).
- Evaluate all the information against your checklist of criteria.

2   Think of the response required and prepare a written brief accordingly

- Prepare a concise but thorough written brief for the competing agencies. It is advisable to clarify if the review is a statutory one.
- It must be clear from the brief whether strategic proposals alone are required, whether some creative ideas or a full creative pitch are expected, or whether a workshop or trial project is envisaged. Agencies should respect the client's wishes in this. Be sensitive to the fact that creative pitches are an expensive and resource draining exercise for agencies.
- Be clear about the nature of the services that you expect to use.
- Indicate proposed remuneration and contract terms. Make the budget explicit from the outset – this is as important as outlining remuneration. This will safeguard against misunderstandings during negotiations.
- Identify and make clear all criteria on which the agencies' presentations will be judged and specify the time allowed for them. If pitches are to take place at your premises, advise agencies on the presentation facilities available, size and nature of meeting room, etc., and allow access in advance.
- No more than 20 agencies should be asked for their response to a preliminary 'due diligence' questionnaire or 'Request for Information' (RFI).
- No more than a maximum of 10 agencies should be asked to make 'long list' standard credentials presentations.
- No more than 6 agencies should be asked to prepare extended credentials or 'think-piece' presentations for short listing.

3   Consider the time necessary for response to the brief

- Prepare a firm timetable for the total pitching or evaluation process and stick to it.
- Allow sufficient time for agencies to have face-to-face meetings with you to discuss the brief, ask questions, and to establish a rapport with you. Don't underestimate the value of informal meetings with the competing agencies.

- If you decide to use a workshop approach, build in sufficient time to implement this process, including scheduling diary time for key personnel involved in the selection team.
- Time must be allowed for development of constructive ideas between brief and presentation. Bearing in mind that full proposals can take weeks or months to develop in an ongoing relationship, four weeks minimum is suggested for the development of work for a full creative pitch. Different pitch approaches, such as extended credentials, 'think-pieces', strategic recommendations, and workshops, can take less time and still be effective.

4   Invite up to three agencies to pitch (or four if incumbent is included)

- Decide positively on a pitch list of up to three agencies only. If the incumbent is invited, the list can go up to four agencies in total.
- Don't invite the incumbent to pitch if you have no intention of re-appointing them. If you haven't already done so, talk to the incumbent about why you are not including them in the shortlist.
- Don't be seduced into lengthening the list.
- Make competing agencies aware of the number of agencies on the pitch list and whether the incumbent is included. The client should confirm in writing whether or not the pitch process and the names of the participants are confidential.
- If there is a requirement for participating agencies to sign non-disclosure or confidentiality agreements, it should be done at this point.

5   Give background market data, interpretation and clarification

- You should be willing to share, on a confidential basis, market data and other relevant research and allow agency personnel access to people in the company with whom they would work if appointed.
- Make sure that there is always a specified senior member of the client's company to handle all enquiries and meet requests of the agency to ensure consistency of response. Don't underestimate the time involved of someone being fully available over a short period of time.
- Allow the same rules of access to all agencies pitching.

6   Help the process by demonstrating commitment with some financial contribution

- You should decide whether to make a monetary contribution to the pitch.
- Some financial contribution (announced upfront and the same offer to all agencies on the shortlist) shows commitment and the seriousness of your intent. The objective is to motivate the agencies and ensure a professional process: the contribution is very unlikely to cover all the third party, staff and associated costs.

7   Understand the roles of all those involved on both sides and set up an objective evaluation system

- Ensure that all the decision-makers have been fully briefed and that they are all present at each stage.

- Advise the agencies of job titles and roles of those attending for the client.
- Establish an objective evaluation system for assessing each pitch.
- Ensure that the agency presentation teams include people who will actually work on the business.

8 Insist on necessary commercial disciplines before an appointment is made

- Ensure that the business side (contracts, remuneration and the management of the relationship) is discussed before an appointment is made. The involvement of marketing procurement professionals in the search process should ensure that terms are negotiated at the right stage and all contractual obligations formally signed.
- Help in the form of model contractual terms and relevant courses is available from the DMA, IPA, ISBA, MCCA and PRCA.

9 Decide and inform quickly and fairly

- Decide on the winning agency as soon as possible, normally no more than one week after all the agency presentations have taken place (except in those special cases where it has been agreed to put competing creative work into research).
- Establish a proper procedure for notifying both successful and unsuccessful agencies of the decision.
- Ensure that all pitching agencies learn of the result on the same day.
- Immediately issue a press release to the trade press.

10 Key guidelines on implementation and relationship management

- After the pitch, give the losing agencies the courtesy of a full 'lost order' meeting. Use the 'feedback form' available online with the full version of this guide.
- Any losing agencies must return all confidential material and information provided for the pitch to you, and you, on request, must return the losing agencies' pitch presentations.
- Honour the incumbent agency's contract, particularly with regard to the agreed notice period and payment of outstanding invoices.
- Ensure that they cooperate fully in a hand-over to the new agency, making sure that all materials belonging to you are handed back in accordance with the contract.
- Once an appointment is made, ensure that a contract between client and agency is actually negotiated, agreed and signed. Contracts must be adhered to throughout the relationship, up to and including termination.
- Welcome the winning agency into the start of a long-lasting and mutually satisfying relationship. Arrange for mutual induction meetings to create familiarity between personnel and with your respective business processes.
- Agree realistic objectives for brand or corporate communications, put measures of effectiveness in place and report key metrics regularly at CEO/main board level.
- Client–agency relationships are valuable and need active management: review and reinvest in the relationship by the strategic use of brainstorms, 'awaydays' and refreshing the team with new people.

Here are some points which I feel are worth stressing in order that you enter the process prepared:

1   It is worth keeping up with the changing face of the agency landscape even when you are not looking. It will then stand you in good stead when you do come back into 'pitch' mode. This can be achieved most effectively through:

   • Keeping an eye on the marketing press.
   • Attending award events.
   • Monitoring the agencies of competitor companies.
   • Attending the Marketing Forum and Communication Directors' Forum annual events.

2   If you are in new territory it will be important to work with a trade body or third-party specialist. In addition, you may still wish to talk to somebody in another company who has recently gone through a similar experience. You can get their details through the above intermediaries.

3   As you can imagine there are horror stories among the agency community about client companies holding 'nightmare' pitches. It is worth remembering in the agency selection process you can enhance or damage your company's brand in the wider marketing arena. Make sure that you create the right impression of professionalism, realistic timings, clear briefs, access to the right people/information, etc.

4   Create a pitch timetable which is realistic for you, your assisting intermediary and the agencies (consider holidays and any important business commitments). Make sure that the key decision-makers are available. This may require you booking time in their diaries well in advance.

5   Understand how your senior management will be involved in the agency selection decision. If they are not 'agency-literate', work out what is the best stage for them to get involved, what their criteria are and what the format of meeting should be.

Source for p62: Finding an Agency – Joint industry guidelines reproduced by permission of DMA, IPA, ISBA, MCCA and the PRCA. Fully downloadable from each of the trade bodies' websites (addresses in the Useful Information Sources section).

6   Be disciplined with yourself in terms of how many agencies you put on the longlists and shortlists. Ask yourself if you and your colleagues really have the time to see so many agencies.

7   You will glean a good deal of information from the agency brochure, showreel and/or website. However there is no substitute for visiting the offices, which will give you a very good impression. Go out of your way to make sure you see the 'real' environment not just the pitch façade.

  • Arrive 10 minutes early and see how they cope.
  • Ask to be given a tour of the agency. (I know that a certain airline, who prided itself on the detail of its customer service, did not consider an agency because their toilets were in such a mess!)
  • Ask on the way to be introduced to a random member of staff (not just the pitch team).

8   Consider a 'last-minute' request in the last 24/48 hours – an additional, reasonable request to the brief which could give an indication of their flexibility and their responsiveness (e.g. a request to think about a new aspect of the campaign and talk about it in the presentation).

9   Always take up references from clients. Also you will learn more through a telephone conversation rather than a one-sided letter or email.

10 Make sure you create a tight brief not a request with reams of unfiltered data.

11 Consider asking a junior colleague to get involved in organizing the logistics of your company's involvement in the pitch process to free up your time a little.

12 Only 10% of pitch work actually runs in the marketplace. Although you may use an artificial brief for purposes of the pitch; choose something that will have implications for future campaigns and/or focuses on a problem you will be facing.

13 Try to construct the pitch so that you can assess the strategic and creative recommendations independently of evaluating the team with whom you will be working on a day-to-day basis.

14 Make sure that you and your colleagues determine (before the pitch presentations start) what the evaluation criteria and the accompanying weightings are. Create an evaluation form (see Figure 3.4) so that, at the

Post-pitch feedback form

Crazy For Work
L I M I T E D

Name of Client company: _____

Name of Client (optional): _____

Name of Agency: _____

Name of Brand/project: _____

Please circle appropriate number	1 Excellent	2 Above expectations	3 Meets expectations	4 Below expectations	5 Unacceptable
Pre-pitch					
Our understanding of the agency in terms of its size, positioning, capabilities and its overall offering was clear prior to our first meeting	1	2	3	4	5
The agency lived up to these expectations at the first credentials meeting	1	2	3	4	5
The agency asked insightful questions and demonstrated a good understanding of our business/market at our first meeting	1	2	3	4	5
We were impressed by the team that we met and felt that the chemistry between us was good	1	2	3	4	5
We felt that there was likely to be a good cultural fit between ourselves and the agency	1	2	3	4	5
Background and objectives					
The agency demonstrated a real understanding of where we are now (the current position of the brand, its background and the key issues it faces and which define the start point for the journey on which communications will take the brand)	1	2	3	4	5
The agency demonstrated a real understanding of where we want to be (the desired destination of the journey on which successful communications need to take our brand in the context of our overall corporate business and marketing plan, as well as of what will be achievable)	1	2	3	4	5
The agency demonstrated a real understanding of what we need to do to get there (in terms of our total marketing programme and the role of communications within it)	1	2	3	4	5
The agency demonstrated a real understanding of how we'll know we've arrived (in terms of setting targets and measures to evaluate their proposed campaign)	1	2	3	4	5

Source: Finding an Agency – Joint industry guidelines reproduced by permission of DMA, IPA, ISBA, MCCA and the PRCA (2004). Fully downloadable from each of the trade bodies' websites (addresses in the Useful Information Sources section).

Figure 3.4   Pitch evaluation form

Post-pitch feedback form

Crazy For Work
L I M I T E D

Please circle appropriate number	1 Excellent	2 Above expectations	3 Meets expectations	4 Below expectations	5 Unacceptable
Customer insight and communications strategy					
The agency demonstrated an in-depth understanding of both our business and our consumers	1	2	3	4	5
Their customer insight was strong and was the basis for powerful brand communications	1	2	3	4	5
The agency defined the role for communications clearly in the context of the brand's overall marketing strategy	1	2	3	4	5
The agency's strategic recommendations clearly addressed the specific issues in our brief	1	2	3	4	5
Creative proposals					
The link between the agency's strategic thinking and the creative idea was strong	1	2	3	4	5
The agency presented a 'big idea' for the brand, which was 'campaignable' and could clearly be delivered through most media and communications channels	1	2	3	4	5
The creative idea appeared to be deliverable in the required timescale and affordable	1	2	3	4	5
Team and presentation					
We had an appropriate amount of contact with the agency team during the pitch process	1	2	3	4	5
We felt the team were committed to our brand / business and would be hardworking and proactive	1	2	3	4	5
We felt that the team would be collaborative and good to work with	1	2	3	4	5
The agency fielded the most appropriate team on the pitch day	1	2	3	4	5
The agency presentation was delivered clearly and professionally	1	2	3	4	5
Our questions were clearly answered	1	2	3	4	5

Figure 3.4 (*continued*)

Post-pitch feedback form

Crazy For Work
L I M I T E D

Please circle appropriate number	1 Excellent	2 Above expectations	3 Meets expectations	4 Below expectations	5 Unacceptable
The agency's presentation documentation was well produced and provided a good summary and rationale for their recommendations	1	2	3	4	5
The agency's post-pitch follow-up was appropriate	1	2	3	4	5

Remuneration

The agency put forward a clear, fair and understandable proposal which seemed likely to incentivize them whilst delivering value for us	1	2	3	4	5

Overall

What did this agency do that was markedly better than the other agencies that were pitching?

_____
_____
_____
_____

What did any/all of the other agencies do that was markedly better than this agency?

_____
_____
_____
_____

What was the single most important factor in this agency winning/not winning the business?

_____
_____
_____
_____

Are there any other comments that you feel would help this agency for future pitches?

_____
_____
_____
_____

Figure 3.4 *(continued)*

end of the presentations, you and your colleagues can discuss them from the same basis.

15 Agencies can be prone to saying what they think clients wish to hear. Dig deeper with your questions. If you want to know how well they work with agencies, do not just ask 'How well do you work with other agencies?' but ask for relevant specific examples from their current work.

16 Look out for tell-tale signs of an agency in an unsettled state – particularly just after or before a merger/takeover. Try to understand the future implications for your business and if they can cope with the inevitable turmoil.

17 Recognize the role you want the required agency to play with your other agencies. Does it have experience of being the 'leader' or 'follower' agency?

18 Make sure that there is formal internal agreement on which agency has won (I have heard of situations where one agency was told it was successful on the Friday and told otherwise on the following Monday). Also make sure you let all the agencies know of the result personally. There have been cases of the non-successful agencies finding out through the press.

19 With all that effort from the non-successful agencies, it is worth making sure you give feedback accordingly, you never know if you may need their help in the future. Interestingly some agencies do not want the feedback, but if they do, do not disguise things by saying that they all came a 'close second'. Give them clear feedback.

20 In the overall process, treat an agency how you would like to be treated.

MEETING THE AGENCY FACE-TO-FACE

The main two meetings in the process, the 'chemistry meeting' and the final presentation are 'crunch' encounters for both sides. The chemistry meeting is designed to allow both teams to get to know each other, size each other up and maybe discuss an issue or some agency case studies that are relevant to the client. It could also be a precursory discussion of the brief to be issued. The final presentation will be imbued with a sense of occasion on both sides, and is the crescendo to the various meetings and the answering of the brief.

The chemistry meeting will be where you will use your instincts as much as anything. Yet you need to be wary of that famous agency charm. Make sure you see substance in their offering. If they say that they like to be a strategic partner to clients, ask them to give examples and ask them to discuss the challenges involved in this. Do not be impressed by creative work without exploring the associated business results. Find the person in the team who has impressive opinions, and understand who will *really* be working with you on a day-to-day basis; allow the agency to air their views and experience.

In the final presentation, watch out for the dynamics of the team – do they work well together? Do they talk over each other? Do they cope well in adversity (failing projection equipment, etc.)? Are they prepared for your questions? Can they keep to the time you allocated? Admittedly, there is no one single indicator that they are the right team for you so you need to score them accordingly (see Figure 3.4) but ask yourself this: *Do they inspire you to approach your marketing more imaginatively?*

In general, what you are looking for in face-to-face meetings is evidence of:

- chemistry (with you and among themselves).
- culture fit.
- agency philosophy and values.
- team depth.
- strategic thinking.
- creative credentials.
- expertise/experience with certain media, brands, market sectors.
- analytical skills.
- communication skills.
- project management skills.
- response to a brief.

COMMENT

Agencies are made up of people and they are what you are really 'buying'. There have been cases where an agency has done better work (which has also researched better) but another agency has won because the client likes the people involved and wants to work with them.

Make sure that in your interaction with the agencies that you have built in enough opportunities to see how the chemistry flows with your team and within their own team. I know of one client whose last stage in the selection process was to take the final two agencies sailing on the Solent on separate days to assess this very point. They could both do the job but it was the human factor that needed to be tested.

They also need to be the right people for your company culture. One client suggested dinner with two prospective agencies and chose the agency who opted for the less glamorous route of inviting the client for a curry. This was just right for the client team and showed a 'down-to-earthness' in the agency team.

POST-PITCH FEEDBACK

Ultimately you will need to make a selection decision based on what you have witnessed from the agencies and the discussion with the decision-making team. In your original discussions with the internal team you will have expressed what you are looking for from an agency and the standards by which you will recognize the agency you wish to appoint. Make sure that these criteria are captured in an evaluation document (see Figure 3.4) and are agreed before the agency interview process starts. You can then use this as a basis for your scoring sheet in the meetings and then when you come to feedback to the agencies, you can share the transparency of your evaluation, in part or as a whole as you so wish.

As already mentioned, it is quite important to share feedback with the agencies who were not successful as not only will the agencies have invested a lot of blood, sweat and tears in the process, but it is human nature to want to know 'why not?' And if you have asked them to invest this effort, time and money speculatively, then they deserve your feedback. It will help them in the construction of their next new business offering and you may also want to stay in touch with them for the future.

EXERCISES

1   Name three other advertisers'/marketers' creative work you admire.

2   Name three agencies whose work you admire.

3   Use the template in Figure 3.2 to gauge your existing agency relation-
    ship issues.

BRIEFING AN AGENCY

CHAPTER 4

BRIEFING AN AGENCY

In this chapter you will learn about:

- The value of a briefing process.
- The role of the different briefing stages.
- The key elements to the brief.
- Four principles for a good brief.
- The hotspots of the brief.
- Developing a challenging communications proposition.
- Creating an inspiring briefing.

You will find that many colleagues and agency partners set a good deal of store by the brief you issue for a campaign. For me the brief is the greatest leverage point by which you can consolidate everybody's expert thinking and influence your customers. Nevertheless, there are many misguided interpretations of how a briefing can work – from the cavalier attitude of a verbal 'brain dump' by the campaign manager to those in agencies who seem to worship at the altar of the Brief (part interventionist-God, part omniscient force that divinely produces creative work). Let's be clear: the brief and the briefing process are the product of people working together, their relentless inquisitiveness and their desire to influence the marketplace in an inspiring and impactful way.

You need to decide what works for your situation but there are some common principles that will run through the different campaign processes. In formal and informal research with both marketing departments and agencies, I have asked what words come to mind when they think of 'briefs'. The results have been textbook-like such as 'focused', 'insightful' and 'succinct', and revealing such as 'scary', 'frightening' and 'hard work'. And this dichotomy is the crux of the problem. Some people know the theory of what a brief should do but are genuinely daunted by the task, so they either avoid it or shortcut the process.

THE VALUE OF THE BRIEFING PROCESS

If we define briefing as a clear set of inspiring instructions on where we are and what we need to achieve, we have to ask what benefits a good briefing brings. Viewed externally, it will lead to better work and a greater impact with a company's target audience. Viewed internally, it will save both time and money in terms of the more efficient use of people and resources. It will, in addition, establish benchmarks not only for your impact on the market but also for your performance and that of your agency partners. (No wonder people say 'scary'!)

I really like the explanation given by Gary Duckworth in the chapter 'Creative Briefing' in *Excellence in Advertising* (Butterfield, 1999). He goes back to school physics lessons and quotes the Archimedean principle, explaining what levers do:

> Archimedes said *'Give me a place to stand and I can move the world'*. He was explaining the concept of leverage, whereby a small force exerted at the right point is magnified through distance to move an immense object. The brief is the place the account team gives the creative team to stand in their quest to move the world – i.e. to shape the decisions and perceptions of the target group out there in the real world.

Gary Duckworth was seeing it once the brief had come into the agency, but earlier in the process you, as the client, also define where the brand and the communications stand when you brief the agency. Getting the brief right at the beginning will lead to greater leverage in the marketplace and consequently stronger business results.

COMMENT

According to the Charted Institute of Marketing (CIM) we are bombarded with at least 1500 messages a day. These could be on posters and T-shirts on our way to work, email spam at the office, direct mail or TV at home, etc. The majority of which tends to be unsolicited.

In this context, the marketing communications you produce need to (1) cut through the clutter, (2) be relevant as well as (3) be motivating. So if your brief to the agency is the starting point of this process, it is also the single most important contribution the marketing team can make to a great campaign. This should not be underestimated.

THE ROLE OF THE DIFFERENT BRIEFING STAGES

Usually there is not just one brief. In companies where there are internal campaign management teams, the product marketing team briefs the internal campaign team who, in turn, briefs the agency who ultimately produces a creative brief for the creative team, as in Figure 4.1.

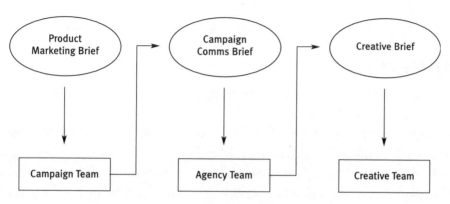

Figure 4.1 Different types of briefs according to different target audiences

It may also be that the campaign communications brief is given to the other agencies involved and briefs may be generated specifically for media or data. Whatever, it is worth bearing in mind that each brief has a different target audience and therefore will require slightly different emphasis. So when the agency sends back a draft creative brief for you to approve, it may have stripped out some information less relevant for the creative team and it will be written in a tone and style relevant for a copywriter and art director. In effect, it is also a potential confirmation of your instructions to the agency so you will need to make sure that it has taken on board your requirements, even if not explicitly stated.

Some people forget that each brief will have a different function and different target audience. What you are trying to achieve at each stage, however, is a progression of thinking. The campaign team (using our example of the three-tier process) takes the product marketing issues and frames them in a communications context (maybe with specific media target audience numbers, relationship to the brand, proposition, etc.). The account team and planner in the agency hone the customer insight, proposition and support to open up potential creative routes. As one moves though the process, there should be more direction, focus and clarity for the creative product.

Something that is very important, and is apparent in the briefing exercises I conduct in the workshops, is *increasing distortion* which can occur in the real day-to day operations. If the first stage of briefing is flawed then the flaw can easily be magnified in the briefs and in the work produced down the line. For example, if there is condescension in the customer description, this disdain will end up either producing arrogant work or, more likely, suppressing successful empathetic approaches. Similarly, if there is lack of clear thinking at the start of the briefing process, this lack of clarity will envelop the other stages of the brief.

COMMENT

Some people have described the briefing process as a relay race where the baton is handed on. Others feel that this is not quite right because it implies that when you have passed on the brief your job is done (which is not the case). I would say it is rather like a relay race where once the team mates have run their stretch, they run at the side of their colleagues and administer encouragement and energy-giving sugar drinks. I may be stretching the analogy but the important point is that the process has different stages where individuals have a significant role to play, but a collaborative framework is needed so that the combined team work together to get the best result.

When you think about what agencies want from a client brief, you should ask your particular agency partners what they specifically want. In an Admap article (*Briefing Creative Agencies* by Roderick White, June 2003) it was stated that they want to 'be informed, guided and challenged – but not set impossible tasks or drowned in paperwork'. That would corroborate the general feeling that client briefs should:

- involve.
- give direction.
- excite.
- inspire.
- not restrict unnecessarily.

THE KEY ELEMENTS TO THE BRIEF

The industry bodies (the IPA, ISBA, MCCA and PRCA) have published joint guidelines (*The Client Brief: A best practice guide to briefing communications agencies*) to help marketers to brief agencies. The guidelines can be downloaded from the respective websites.

The key section headings in the guidelines for a best practice brief are:

1   Project Management (e.g. date, project name, project type, purchase order number, job number, brand company name, client team and contact details, agency team and contact details).
2   Where are we now? (e.g. current status of brand, background, key issues facing communications, product attributes, distribution, market size, customer usage data, the brand's positioning, competitive activity).
3   Where do we want to be? (i.e. single-minded, measurable objective).
4   What are we doing to get there? (i.e. marketing strategy, campaign strategy).
5   Who do we need to talk to?
6   How will we know we have arrived? (i.e. measures).
7   Practicalities (e.g. budgets, timings, brand guidelines, structures).
8   Approvals.

There is also an interactive online tool that guides you through the whole brief writing process. You can see it at www.clientbrief.info.

COMMENT

As we go through the different elements of the brief, there is an underlying assumption that the brief will be written. Yet I know that this is not always the case even with blue-chip companies. Look at these quotes from some interviews I did with a particular marketing department:

> '. . . I'll just download for half and hour and let the agency worry about it. But, then the problem is that when they come back, once they've been through it again, you can't go back to your original points and make sure that they've been taken on board . . .'

> '. . . I'm pretty sure what criteria I'm supposed to be evaluating the work against but god knows what criteria the others are using when there is no brief. . .'

It shows that they know that there will be problems down the line yet they are not disciplined enough to save themselves, and their colleagues, time, money and personal stress.

Written briefs give you:

1 Clarity and focused thinking.
2 Progression of logical thinking.
3 Focus for approval process and confirmation of internal buy-in.
4 Time and money savings.
5 Easier project handovers.
6 Confirmation of campaign measurement.

FOUR PRINCIPLES FOR A GOOD BRIEF

All briefs should demonstrate evidence of:

- Understanding the brand.
- Achieving clarity.

- Maintaining focus.
- Creating surprise.

Understanding the Brand

Some companies have brand departments to maintain the integrity of the established brand and aid its development as the company evolves. Other companies would not necessarily see that they have a 'brand'. I would contend that even your plumber has a brand to understand, protect and invest in. So what is a brand? Where do you start and stop with this definition? Seen from the side of the manufacturer or service provider, it is a *promise in the marketplace*; and for the customer, it is a *set of perceptions and associations* in his/her mind linked to that promise. There are different terms associated with a brand and, in running the risk of confusing terminology, here are some definitions that may help you to express your brand and marketplace presence. My advice is to make sure that you and the agency standardize these terms to avoid any future misunderstandings.

Identity   A visual and tone of articulation of the company/product/service.
Positioning   How you want customers to think of you and see you
                differently from your competition.
Proposition   The offer or offering to the marketplace.
Attribute   The tangible tool at the brand's disposal to differentiate it
                physically.
Personality   The proprietary character and tone of voice.

[*NB*: Some people confuse a strapline with a proposition. This is because a strapline on an ad is a public expression of the brand/campaign proposition. They are not, however, exchangeable terms.]

Ever since 1827 when Bass first used the term 'brand', marketers have been arguing internally within companies how to use the brand to the greatest effect. To enable you to use your brand most effectively for the brief and the subsequent creative work, you need to know the answers to these questions:

1   What do we want the brand to stand for?
2   What does the brand currently stand for?
3   How is our brand different from its competitors?
4   How does our brand talk to people?

Everything in the brief must be consistent with the brand as this is the opportunity to leverage the power of the brand and all communications should contribute to the brand. The lighthearted legal terms and conditions of the Virgin Mobile telephone service are a good example. ('Why does everyone quote Virgin?' I hear you groan. Watch out as I am going to mention them again in later pages.) It shows how a mobile telephone company can springboard off the mother brand values (as the consumers' champion, slightly irreverent, giving value for money, etc.) and take it down to the very small detail of the legalese you receive with the delivery of the phone, showing that even legal departments can sometimes have a sense of humour.

Achieving Clarity

Vagueness in a brief breeds misunderstanding. If the brief is not clear, there's little chance that the agency response will be what you want. You may not be actually ready to formulate the brief if you cannot be clear enough. Here are some ways to improve clarity in the brief:

1   Re-think, re-question (leave it after first draft and then come back to it; share it with a colleague).
2   Use plain English and avoid jargon (our world is full of marketing speak, root this out; do not use company-idiosyncratic acronyms).
3   Keep it simple (think about how you would explain it to someone at the coffee machine or your Mum or Dad).
4   Check for contradictions (there should be a generic thread running through the brief – it should be a story that builds).
5   Avoid misunderstandings (maybe a 'Question and Answer' session internally and then with the agency).

6   Avoid cutting and pasting from previous briefs (we have all been guilty of this, but it is the one single biggest cause of unclear briefs).

Maintaining Focus

In practice, people find it hard to take in one point from a piece of communications, let alone two. If we have, as stated earlier, some 1500 commercial messages fighting for our daily attention, you can appreciate why communications need to be single-minded. Focus can be achieved through:

1   Agreeing on one simple communications objective and one message.
2   Describing exactly what you want the customer to do as a response to the communications.
3   Filtering out any extraneous information.
4   Identifying relevance to audience.

Creating Surprise

We mostly operate in a very 'me-too' marketplace. Customers have heard your sales pitch before – to make them take notice, you must approach it from a new angle. As a colleague says 'surprise them or lose them'. Surprise can be achieved in a number of ways in a brief by:

1   Identifying what everyone else in the marketplace is doing and doing it differently.
2   Doing what you have been doing differently.
3   Seeing the world from a different angle (maybe not even your customer's viewpoint, e.g. 'how would my children react to this?').
4   Taking another marketer's approach (e.g. if you are in the car market, ask yourself how Paul Smith, the outfitter, would approach your marketplace).
5   Researching and developing a new insight about your target audience.

COMMENT

What is a customer insight? Everybody's talking about insights. A customer insight is a penetrating discovery about a customer's motivation designed to unlock an impactful assault on their senses. When the US marketing team who was responsible for developing a new campaign for promoting milk sales approached the brief, they decided to find a new angle other than the usual 'milk – it's good for you' health perspective. They created their 'surprise' factor by employing *deprivation research*, which is where you pay consumers to go without your product and keep a diary of their actions. One of the quotes from the discussion at the end of the deprivation period indicated a new angle to the attraction of milk: *'I didn't know what to do. I thought about drinking some and coming here and lying, but that wouldn't have been right. So then I thought maybe I should come clean, but then perhaps you'd throw me out and I wouldn't get paid. So I put the milk back. And the cookies just weren't the same. Actually it was a bad end to a bad day.'* Not only does it show the American link with milk and cookies, it reveals a relationship with milk which is not just about healthiness. When that relationship is terminated, people start to appreciate milk more. So the insight was – people do not value milk very highly until they run out of it. This led to the incredibly successful 'Got Milk' campaign. (Read the full story in *Truth, Lies and Advertising* by Jon Steel, 1998.)

For me, surprise is the X factor in the impact. Think of those physical safety demonstrations on aircraft where the passengers do not pay any attention and airline staff look embarrassed about the whole ritual. Well, in the case of Virgin Atlantic, they have taken the surprise element of animation and humour and have created a very sweet but attention-grabbing cartoon that really gets the message across. Its soundtrack by Mr Scruff and its understanding of human nature make it very watchable. It is regularly praised in in-flight reviews and it does not expose the personnel to embarrassment or make them look like naughty schoolchildren. It shows that if you approach things differently you can find a more innovative solution to an everyday task which then gets noticed.

THE HOTSPOTS OF THE BRIEF

There are some areas of the brief on which it is worth spending more time as they cause the most problems but can ultimately give the most benefit:

- The objective of the communications (where do we want to be?).
- The customers (who do we need talk to?).
- The proposition and support (what message do we want to communicate?).

The Objective of the Communications

In defining what you are trying to achieve with the communications, make sure that an objective is SMART:

Specific   Objectives need to be clear and articulate what is expected in terms of what, by when, where and by how much.

Measurable   If you cannot measure an objective, you will not know whether you have achieved it.

Achievable   Objectives need to be realistic. They can be slightly aspirational but definitely achievable. This will maintain motivation.

Relevant   Objectives need to relate correctly to the overall vision so that the latter can be achieved.

Time related   There must be starting and ending points so that those involved are aware of time constraints.

An example of a sales objective would be 'To increase online sales of the flagship cookery book in December by 30% compared to those of last year'. The communications objective could be 'To raise awareness of online purchase of cookery book by 10% in November and December'.

The Customers

Certain internal departments are very good at supplying sales data and basic demographics, but what is lacking is the information that brings the customer to life in your eyes and in the eyes of the agency's creative team. Stronger insight will also allow a better understanding of the approach to be taken, the tone of voice and any differentiated messages that need to be communicated. Ask yourself these questions:

1   Who am I talking to? (age, family status, at home/at work, etc . . .)
2   What are they like? (likes, dislikes, purchases, behaviour)

3   What is the relationship with my brand/product?
4   Why do they feel like that?
5   How do they feel about my competitors?
6   How does my product/service fit into their lives?

TIP

Do not think of them as an 'audience', as that presupposes that they are listening (to all those 1500 daily messages!). Try to think of them as individual real people living in the real world.

Try to make sure that you meet as many of your customers as possible – either in a business environment (Lexus marketers have to spend time in dealerships and a regular stint in the Customer Relations department handling customer calls) or in different circumstances (understanding twentysomething games fanatics might be best at games fairs or in the pub).

Let's take a longstanding but still relevant example of turning a demographic portrait into a vivid description which allows a potential insight:

Van Drivers: C2/D men 25–55 years old

This could be written as White Van Men – everybody in the UK marketing world would know what is meant by this but (1) there is implied disdain with this term which will not help the creative process (to paraphrase David Ogilvy, in his assertion that you should always empathize with your customers, the customer is not a moron. He's your brother!) and (2) there is no particular insight that leads onto a proposition. Seeing them differently helps:

'They are one-man bands who work incredibly hard to get the job done, battling through roadworks to get to the pipes before the pipes burst. Although they will tell you their life is a treadmill and a trial, they secretly savour their unsung heroism. They expect the van to be the same as them (tough and uncomplaining). They are not particularly aware of ABC as a van manufacturer. Those who are aware, don't consider ABC vans to be particularly solid or tough.'

This can lead to an insight such as: *If their van lets them down, they lose money.*

The Proposition and Support

The area that creates most tension is that of the proposition and support, so we shall explore this more fully in the next section.

DEVELOPING A CHALLENGING COMMUNICATIONS PROPOSITION

Clients and agencies alike say that the proposition and support is the hardest area of the brief to complete satisfactorily. In fact, along with the target market this is the area from which the creative team look for inspiration. So we have universal acceptance that it is difficult, but if the proposition is just developed in isolation, it will never get easier. It should be seen as a culmination of planning, customer research and further combined thinking. The proposition should be a single-minded thought which inspires customers to re-evaluate things and potentially do something specific. It is the essence of what will be communicated. It should be a simple, surprising statement that can cut through people's clutter/cynicism/indifference/hostility.

Make sure your proposition conforms to the 'Proposition Checklist':

- Is it single-minded?
- Is it surprising, thought-provoking, motivating?
- Is it relevant to the customer and the brand?
- Will someone be convinced by it more than the competitors?
- Can you explain it to a mate?
- Can you imagine a headline being developed from this?

A good example of a great proposition is from HHCL when they were working on the AA. In fact it was an art director rather than the planner who connected some thinking and came up with 'The AA – it's like the fourth emergency service'.

It is always worth taking time to devise a genuinely strong proposition. Try to formulate it in a way that is interesting and exciting. I think it was again David Ogilvy – talking about the seminal Rolls-Royce ad ('At 60 miles an hour the loudest noise in this new Rolls-Royce comes from the electric clock') – who described interrogating the product until it confesses its strengths. This kind of rigour of thinking can be seen in the way the next proposition has been developed:

> *Explore the product truths . . .*
> Every year BA carries 12 million people.
>
> *Follow the argument through . . .*
> Every year BA carries 12 million people to other people.
>
> *Find the consumer benefit . . .*
> BA brings more people together than any other airline.

In this case, the product truth becomes support for the inspiring proposition.

Recently HSBC has taken that same type of 'big is small' thinking and translated it into their proposition of 'being a huge international bank makes you everyone's local bank'.

When looking at the support (i.e. the reason why customers should believe in the proposition), remember that it should only contain facts/information relevant to the task. It should be credible and motivating to the customer. It should logically link to the proposition. It is not a dumping ground for general information. In fact, try to dig around for interesting support as it is often that which provides the greatest springboard for creativity.

TIP

Rome was not built in a day and definitely not alone. Firstly, do not see the task of brief-writing as a sole undertaking – shared thinking is better thinking. Share your initial draft with a colleague or your account director/planner. In addition, give it the 'overnight test' in terms of logic, clarity and focus. An inspiring brief is more likely to be created by giving yourself more time and the brief more consideration. This is one of the things that has helped some of my recent clients feel that they are producing substantially better briefs.

Figure 4.2 is a disguised example of a campaign brief which a client worked on with the agency planner. Although it is not necessarily typical, it has a thread of inspiration running through it which creates a sense of excitement about the launch.

Campaign Brief

Brand:	Prismband Broadband
Campaign Name:	Spring Push
Media:	Posters, press, web, direct mail
Brief Writer:	Sarah Banania, Marketing
Date:	10th October 2009
Budget:	€2m ex. VAT
Campaign Period:	Quarter 1
Purchase Order:	Q12590

Inspiration

What does the brand stand for and what is its tone of voice?

Prismband Broadband is about positive intensity of experience: the full-on hit of thrilling speed, vivid colours and vibrant sound. It is the Alton Towers of telecommunications, making the competition look like a rainy afternoon in Skegness. Our tone is full of excitement and optimism, almost child-like: we can't wait to share our new toys with our friends (i.e. customers). This is backed by our pledge to our customers to offer outstanding service.

What precisely must this communication achieve?

To shout aloud about the launch of the new Prismband Broadband offering. It must inspire prospects to become interested enough in Prismband and understand that it is a new force to be reckoned with.

Who exactly are we talking to?

See attached target group breakdowns with geographical and potential income splits.
We are talking to internet-savvy SMEs and SoHo businesses as well as early adopter types amongst the residential population. Likely to have only a basic knowledge of broadband technology and likely to be heavy internet users. They already have broadband but have experienced poor service.

What do we know about them/the product/the market that will help inspire great work?

Our target audience is keen to be at the leading edge of communications, especially where the internet is concerned. Prismband Broadband products are absolutely leading edge. The residential package includes 4 Mb per second broadband (vs 512 Kbps for a standard broadband connection) plus 2 or 3 phone lines for voice (full number portability) – all down the customer's existing single copper cable (which Prismband would take over from the competition). The business package includes 8 Mbps broadband and up to 15 phone lines also down the existing single copper cable. Phone clarity is better than the present competitive product. Taken together, this means faster data and more, clearer voice connections than with the competition for less money: i.e. more intense experiences.

What do we want them to think, feel or do as a result of this communication?

To feel excited and provoked, to think that Prismband is an exciting, energetic cutting-edge player and to call Prismband or visit their website for more information.

What's the single most important message that we want to get across?

With Prismband life and business are more positively intense experiences.

Why should they believe it?

1) The greater speed of Prismband Broadband
2) The greater number of phone lines you can install for the comparative price/capability
3) The fact that all our communications and interactions with customers are vivid and high energy
4) The fact that Prismband (non-broadband) has won consumer service awards this year

Figure 4.2   Sample campaign brief

Campaign Brief

Information

What is the relevant background information to the product/brand?

Prismband has been offering simple telecoms to consumers for some years. Now with Local Loop Unbundling, Prismband can put its own superior equipment into the exchange and into customers' homes/premises, connected to its own superior 'backbone' network, thus enabling it to massively upgrade the amount of data and voice traffic that can be squeezed down the copper cable. With Crazy For Work Limited now owning Prismband, the resources are available to scale up the drive for new customers.
See attached product presentation for specific details of product.

Is this communication part of a bigger marketing campaign? If so, how does it fit with the other activity?

We require the agency to develop an integrated campaign including brand and response-focused elements: posters, press, web and direct mail. Media agency to confirm plan.

How does the communication need to be tailored?

Clearly there is a BtoB element (SMEs) as well as a BtoC element (SoHo, Early adopter residential) – though we wish to avoid a sense of two campaigns. Let's pitch our campaign at the kind of business people and consumers who really welcome the internet/communications revolution and 'get it'. Architects, not accountants. That way our campaign style will work for all. However, within both residential and business prospects there will be more and less tech-savvy customers, so we might want to consider two versions for each – the tech-savvy version containing a more technical feel/information.
See direct mail addendum for specific audience messages.

What secondary message/information do we need to include?

Although we are not selling the brand on price, the ability to bundle a number of phone lines plus keen broadband pricing does create a very affordable offer – typical savings will be around €15 per month versus the nearest competitor equivalent. But this will never be a cheap way to get on the net, or the cheapest way to get broadband – it's just amazing value for a premium service.

What are the exact response devices?

Phone 0800 123456 and web (www.prismband.co.uk) on responsive media.

What are the creative or technical guidelines and constraints?

Prismband corporate guidelines.

How will we know if the campaign has been successful?

Monthly awareness tracking and weekly response analysis from call centre.

Approvals

Bill Heathrow, MD

Tim Gadfly, Product Marketing

Figure 4.2   (*continued*)

CREATING AN INSPIRING BRIEFING

Once I was invited by a junior-level client to travel on a train for two hours and have the brief (which had already been emailed to me and my colleague) read out by the client to us verbatim. The meeting was finished in a maximum of 30 minutes. We got back on the train for another two-hour journey. I still regard it as one of my most uninspiring briefings as it was the opposite of what a briefing session should be. Any briefing session should be designed to *direct and inspire* the agency, *progress the thinking* and *initiate the constant creative dialogue* between the agency and client. The briefing should be:

- an opportunity to discuss and debate the task.
- a chance to review competitive communications.
- a chance to review previous communications and learnings.
- an opportunity to think about the broader picture.
- an opportunity to consult with other agencies/departments.

It should *not* be:

- the first chance to read the written brief.
- an alternative to a clear, well thought-through written brief.

Suggestions for successful briefings include:

- Distribution of the brief before the meeting to ensure a more informed discussion (very important).
- Preparation for the meeting. (What do you need to share at the session? Are there any good stories, insights, anecdotes?) (very important).
- Not reading through the brief section by section in a semi-verbatim way. (Show that you know your subject by telling them 'the story' referring to the brief but not being a slave to it.)
- Bringing an expert/'consumer'/outsider along.
- Holding it in an inspiring location. (Did the Speedo briefing really happen in a swimming pool? We definitely briefed an Art Fund Campaign in the National Portrait Gallery and a colleague held a picnic briefing in the Mercedes MPV – they bring the issues to life.)

COMMENT

Some campaign briefs have a 'creative starters for ten' section where campaign managers are encouraged to put their headlines/concepts into the ring for initial inspiration. I am not sure how comfortable people feel with this. Yet, it does raise an issue worth mentioning. If you have seen an ad on TV or some competitor materials that you have in your head (and believe that they have some relevance) when briefing the agency, share your thoughts with the agency. This way, at least the agency knows about the ads and can either consider or discount them and ultimately, at concept presentation, you do not feel disappointed with the agency not having been able to read your mind.

In essence, briefing an agency is just the start of the dialogue, but spending time on the brief and the briefing will save time at a later stage. I alluded at the beginning of this chapter to my personal belief that some agency people can hold the brief too much in awe. It is definitely the most important process/document before the creative process starts, but it is worth bearing in mind that the thinking and the relentless pursuit of an innovative marketing approach need to continue past approval of the brief – on both sides of the fence.

EXERCISES

1 Think who you would consult after drafting a brief.

2 Develop your own proposition checklist and have it laminated for regular use. Stick it on your pin board.

3 Ask your agency whether it is time to refresh the briefing forms/process.

CHAMPIONING THE CREATIVE PRODUCT

CHAPTER 5

CHAMPIONING THE CREATIVE PRODUCT

In this chapter you will learn about:

- How to evaluate creative.

- Providing usable feedback.

- Creating a creatively receptive environment.

- Presenting creative effectively.

O ther departments in your organization may think that those in marketing just swan around with pretty pictures and polyboard. They may think you hang out with the agency too much, talk about the company's brand a bit too reverently and have no real exposure to the sales 'coalface'. Relax, that's just an occupational hazard – really, what else would they have to rib you about? However, a number of departments such as sales, distribution, development, legal and finance need to be involved in helping you to get your creative product to market. Therefore your role internally becomes one of presenter, diplomat, politician, educationist, PR agent and a host of other tasks not in your job description. Championing the creative product, which will ultimately become your customer communications, starts with making sure you are happy with the creative output the agency is delivering initially and then helping it to survive in your company's processes and approvals. The evaluation stage on your part is key but the work is also dependent on a creatively receptive environment and your passion and commitment to progress things through the various gateways.

HOW TO EVALUATE CREATIVE

Evaluating creative is one of the hardest areas of your job and yet potentially the most rewarding. It has been described as the element that makes people feel part of a wider team because they feel their contribution is typified by their individual evaluation skills. In contrast, it makes certain people run for cover because they feel very uncomfortable about making decisions about the creative product. And somewhere in between there are those who just use their gut instinct to make major market-influencing decisions. In a recent conversation someone summed up this whole area: *'I think anyone can look at creative work and have an opinion – that doesn't mean you're being objective and evaluating it . . . this is where many of us really struggle – what are we supposed to be evaluating this work against?'*

You could say that evaluation starts long before you see the actual work. Accordingly you need to concentrate on:

1 Preparing the groundwork.
2 Determining your evaluation criteria.
3 Establishing the right mindset.

Preparing the Groundwork

Let's go back to the issue of the brief to the agency. Ultimately there will be some discussion about your brief and they will come back with their creative brief which is both a confirmation of their interpretation of your brief and a progression of thinking distilled into a document destined for the creative department. Remember the following questions when you are assessing and appraising the brief:

- Do I agree with the role of communications?
- Does the target audience description feel right and insightful?
- Do I agree with the desired takeout?
- Do I feel the single-minded proposition will achieve that desired takeout?
- Do I agree with the call to action and accompanying benchmarks of success?

TIP

You may want a brief to state the level of finish for the materials that will be presented to you (see the Concept Development section on page 42). If you know that you will have to present this to less 'creatively literate' colleagues, you may wish to flag that the visuals need to be of a high finish. Considering the time a high level of finish requires (e.g. TV animatics), it may be better to be presented with black and white visuals initially and then build in time for further development before these are presented. However, remember to tell the agency that you will need two stages of finish to enable them to gear up for this requirement.

COMMENT

This has been said before but it is essential. Any of your colleagues who will have a say in the approval process of the creative work need to have been previously made aware of the brief. Otherwise they may take issue with the proposition when they see it expressed as a creative work, rather than take issue with the creative work.

Additionally if you and/or your colleagues are aware of any restrictions or mandatory requirements, you need to make sure that the agency has taken these on board.

Determining your Evaluation Criteria

Certain organizations such as Unilever, P&G and the COI have standardized evaluation criteria by which all campaign teams/product marketers need to measure the creative product. Some of the FMCG ones presumably sprang out of a more scientific approach to measuring advertising once out in the marketplace, which was developed in the USA. Methodologies such as ARS Persuasion® informed the belief that a TV ad, for example, needed to (1) demonstrate the product in use, (2) have the product on screen for more than one-third of the commercial, (3) make the product benefit the main message ad and (4) demonstrate the results of use. (This style of ad design could be seen in the 1960s/1970s soap powder commercials.) In this manner, creative work was evaluated by checking off the different elements present in the ad.

As thinking has moved on in terms of market success and communications design, evaluation criteria have evolved to incorporate thoughts on brand differentiation, customer insight, simplicity of message and an individual company's approach to marketing and the marketplace.

Whether your company has a standardized evaluation form or not, you need to know what your evaluation criteria are before the agency presents to you. Your mental checklist for the creative product could incorporate some of the following areas:

- Does it contain an inspiring idea?
- Is it on brief?
- Is it on brand and strategy?
- Does it display the right tone of voice and personality?
- Does it add value to the brand?
- Is it clear who we are talking to?
- Is the message clear?
- Is the point made as simply and as powerfully as possible?
- Does the message come over as relevant and accessible?
- Is it original?
- Does it differentiate your product/service/company?
- Does it have drama, emotion and passion?
- Can the customer see the benefit quickly?
- How would you expect customers to respond to it?
- Could it work in a campaign series? (Is it campaignable?)
- Could it work in other media?
- Is it legal/compliant with ASA/FSA, etc.?
- Will it be on budget/possible in the time?

- Is it feasible?
- What is your gut reaction?

The first point of the checklist is incredibly salient. Does it contain a big idea – something that interprets the proposition and strikes at the hearts and minds of the customers in an inspiring way? David Ogilvy said that unless your advertising contains a big idea, it will pass like a ship in the night! It is the factor that will motivate your customers and allow your colleagues to grasp what you want to achieve with the communications. It will also be the basis for understanding the 'campaignability' and approving the execution at a later date.

Take, for example, the idea in the work we did for the National Art Collections Fund. The Art Fund is an arts charity which helps such organizations as the Victoria & Albert Museum, Tate and the National Gallery with purchasing works of art so that they can remain on public display. An award-winning piece of work came directly out of the proposition: 'The Art Fund keeps art on public display.' The piece of work was actually an installation at Tate Modern, which was a simulation of a picture having been on the wall at Tate but had now been removed. (You could see the marks a picture had left.) This was 'on display' at the time of the Warhol exhibition, opposite Rodin's sculpture of *The Kiss* which the Art Fund had helped to purchase. The strong idea was encapsulated in the thought that without the Art Fund a lot of the nation's gallery walls would be empty (a gallery-type plaque explained this and the work of the Art Fund).

Another installation at the National Gallery was done exploiting the same idea but using a street artist recreating *The Rokeby Venus* next to the line 'Without the Art Fund, this is the closest you'd get to Velázquez's *The Rokeby Venus*'. Both pieces can be seen in Figure 5.1.

TIP

Design your own evaluation form if your department does not have one (see Figure 5.2). It may be that other colleagues or group companies do have such a form but there is no standardized pattern so ask around to see what they use.

When you are designing the form make sure you know the evaluation criteria of the colleagues you will ultimately present to.

Try not to use it in the agency creative presentation as though you were a time and motion expert with a clipboard and a white coat, but use it discreetly or

Source: Reproduced by permission of Partners Andrews Aldridge and the National Art Collections Fund, 2004.

Figure 5.1 'Missing Picture' at Tate Modern and 'Street Art' outside the National Gallery

Creative Evaluation Form

Crazy For Work
LIMITED

Campaign title: _____
Medium used: _____
Agency involved: _____

On strategy	- Will it achieve the communications objective?	☐
On proposition	- Does it correspond to the proposition in the brief?	☐
On brand	- How does it leverage the brand? - How does it add to the brand?	☐
On TOV	- Does it have the right tone of voice?	☐
Big Idea	- Is there a big idea here?	☐
Campaignable	- Can you see it working across other treatments and other media?	☐
Insightful	- Does it exploit the key insight about the customer?	☐
Benefit-led	- Are the key benefits exposed?	☐

Is it?
　☐ Simple
　☐ Clear
　☐ Relevant
　☐ Impactful

Is it?
　☐ Involving
　☐ Informing
　☐ Inspiring

Next Action: _____
_____
_____

Figure 5.2　Sample creative evaluation form

mentally and perhaps after the meeting when you have time and space to think about things.

Remember, the idea of an evaluation form is not to restrict the creative product. You do not have to tick all the boxes – but you need to be able to understand the relative importance of the criteria and make judgements as to whether the creative idea needs to conform to the various parameters.

Establishing the Right Mindset

Attending an agency creative presentation as the commissioning client is like participating in those reality TV home decoration programmes where householders leave their house to be 'made-over' by a team of designers and gardeners. There is a mixture of anticipation and excitement, tinged with caution and slight dread. Even though the householders know they are in the hands of experts, they are not 100% sure of (1) how their wishes will have been interpreted, (2) how well they will understand and appreciate the new approach and (3) how they and others will react. I think there are some similarities with your context here and the only way to be true to what you really feel is giving yourself the scope to make as good a decision as you can. I am not sure there is such a thing as the *right* decision in these circumstances, so think about the following to help you to evaluate the situation as objectively as possible:

- Give yourself the time and space.
- Decide who you are (see below).
- Give the work respect.
- Have an opinion.

When I talk about giving yourself time and space I mean before, during and after the presentation. First of all, try to make sure that you have scheduled enough time for the meeting (if in doubt, ask the agency how long it needs). You then need to enter the meeting in an emotionally prepared state.

TIP

Do not walk into a creative presentation straight from a heavy previous meeting. Ideally you should empty your head of all those irrelevant concerns before you enter the room. Also, leave other conversations with the agency, such as those about invoicing and missed deadlines, to the end of the meeting.

You should also let the agency know that you will give some initial 'gut feel' feedback but you will need time to consider things and maybe also share things with other colleagues.

'Deciding who you are' is not some existential question you should have answered when reading Jean-Paul Sartre in your teens. You often go into creative presentations wearing a number of metaphorical 'hats'; you often respond in different modes – as marketing strategist, target audience, company politician and/or as you, the individual. The trick is to leave your own personal and company prejudices at the door and try to see the creative idea more from the viewpoint of the customer and the intended communications strategy.

As a strategist you are looking at the work in terms of:

- Is it on brief/brand/proposition?
- Is it distinctive?

As the target audience, you are looking at the work in terms of:

- Do I 'get' the work straightaway?
- What does it give me?
    - A new way of looking at the brand?
    - Entertainment?
    - Flattery?
    - Intellectual satisfaction?
    - A call to action?
    - An incentive to respond?

Also what insight about me, the target audience, does the work draw upon?

- Am I inspired and motivated by the idea?
- What does it ask me to do – is it reasonable?

As a company employee and marketer, you are looking at the work in terms of:

- Have we done anything like this before?
- Is the work on brand guidelines?
- Can it be produced within the timeline and the budget?

As an individual, your obvious question is 'Do I like it or not?' Your gut feel will always be there and some of it comes from you as an individual rather than from your business experience. Gut feel can be good but this area of personal like/dislike needs to be balanced and set against more of the 'objective' criteria (strategy/target audience issues). Perhaps you could use the axes shown in Figure 5.3.

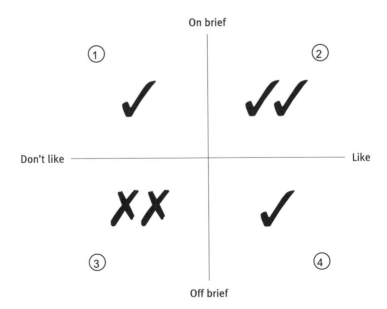

Figure 5.3   Simple creative evaluation axes

If your evaluation appears in Quadrant 2, you are 'cooking' – you have found something which not only meets the brief but about which you have an instinctive feel. If it is in Quadrant 1, examine why you do not like it; explore what you really think in order to decide if there is a problem or if it is personal prejudice. With the second Art Fund campaign, I personally did not like the choice of *The Rokeby Venus* as subject material for the 'Street Art' but had to concede (eventually) that, considering its popularity and its connection to the National Gallery, it was the most appropriate work.

If it is in Quadrant 4, consider changing the strategy if it is a powerful and potentially effective idea. In the case of 'Missing Picture', the concept came out of a brief for a press-dominated campaign. Obviously we still needed press ads but we saw the merit of the ambient idea and implemented it accordingly.

Finally, if you are in Quadrant 3, you and the agency have to face up to the fact that it is back to the drawing board for the creative team. This is the hardest scenario but I think it helps to go through the work with the agency team to discuss why it has failed. Hopefully then the creative team can avoid the same pitfalls.

Whatever quadrant the creative work falls in, you should always give the work *respect*. By this I mean irrelevant of whether it is on/off brief and you dislike/like it, you should appreciate that time and effort has gone into it. You owe it to the work and its originators to evaluate it in a valid way. There are the stories (particularly in pitches) of work being shown in meetings where there have been constant distractions or clients who just say they hate something but will not give any explanation of their dislike. On a practical level, if it is a non-pitch brief, then ultimately you are going to have to work with the agency team further, so it makes sense to give the work respect whether it is a success or not. And I do not mean pandering to any creative preciousness – you can be frank without being unprofessional.

You should also be prepared to have an opinion. This is when you engage with the work and state your reactions. It does not negate the time and space you need to evaluate things at a later date. It shows you are giving work respect, helps the agency to gauge whether it is on the mark or not and allows you to experiment with your evaluation criteria. For me it is a way of talking out aloud.

TIP

You can engage with the work by asking clarifying questions. They will illuminate your thinking and buy yourself a bit more time before you respond to the idea. Also look for clues in the brief. For example, the idea of the Art Fund 'Missing Picture' came straight from interpreting the proposition in a very literal way.

In summary, you should approach evaluating the work by:

- Coming prepared.
- Responding to the idea first (not some minor point).
- Noting your gut reaction but coming back to it later.
- Checking for understanding.
- Asking about the thinking behind the idea.
- Understanding the idea vs the execution.
- Asking clarifying not criticizing questions (maybe more 'how?' than 'why?').
- Showing enthusiasm if you feel it.
- Discussing how it could motivate the customer.
- Exploring 'campaignability', the potential for other executions, possibly in different media.
- Exploring execution.
- Framing your comments in a positive way.

TIP

If you are looking for ways to inform your creative opinion:

- Peruse the IPA Advertising Effectiveness Awards for campaigns that work.
- Read your sector's/discipline's awards supplements.
- Read magazines such as *Campaign*, *Marketing*, etc., for the personal review sections.
- Visit relevant event/seminars.
- Invite your agency's creative director to take you and your colleagues through some interesting and challenging work.
- Talk to more experienced colleagues.
- Read articles and books by marketing/advertising industry figureheads.

PROVIDING USABLE FEEDBACK

When you have to give feedback on concepts to the agency it is important to spend a few minutes thinking of what you are going to say rather than just jumping on the phone unprepared. Clear instructions can save a good deal of time, and the principles worth bearing in mind are:

- Highlight the positive.
- Identify how you feel about the core idea.
- Leave minor points about the execution to later in the conversation.
- Articulate the problem. Do not anticipate the solution.
- Be honest.
- Do not direct what the changes should be.

The feedback can be good or bad but clarity is essential in both cases. I also think that it is worth being positive at the beginning as it sets the tone of the whole conversation – not a token 'I really liked it but everyone else hated it' but things that they can recognize as true rather than 'soft soap'. For example: 'You really came at it using the new customer insight' or 'I thought it had a strong impact at the end of the copy'.

In your preparation, you should check the core idea against the proposition and accompanying support to see how it stacks up. If there is a problem, you will need to be clear about what it is.

In explaining the problem, you can easily stray into the area of suggesting how it should be solved and what the changes should be. This is a tricky area as I do not think it is bad to discuss in the abstract what different scenarios could be, but you have to leave the agency to decide how to rectify the situation. Not only is it the agency's area of expertise but it follows the laws of human nature. Someone once said in another context 'In baiting a trap with cheese, make sure you leave enough room for the mouse'. It is not as cynical as it sounds – for me, in this case, you need to allow the agency enough scope to operate while giving clear direction. There is an example of giving feedback to an agency in the section about 'Talking to the agency about problems with a concept' on page 130.

COMMENT

You may use research to enhance your creative product. Research is a valuable way of ensuring that a campaign is robust for the marketplace. There are different types including creative materials research in qualitative focus groups. Here, there is a word of warning: do not let this type of group determine the concept you should run if you are undecided and want another opinion. This is because you will not necessarily just get one opinion, you could get many contradictory views. Therefore you may not know any more than you did before. This type of group is best to identify the customer issues that can be fed into the creative briefing and afterwards when you have a creative treatment, these groups can help you to fine-tune the communications.

As with any research, commissioning customer research does not absolve you of the responsibility of using your judgement to interpret the findings wisely. Research companies are not oracles but conduits to the voices in the marketplace.

CREATING A CREATIVELY RECEPTIVE ENVIRONMENT

Once you are happy with the concept from the agency, part of your role is to progress it through your organization for approval. A good creative idea will survive the rigours of the internal approval process if you operate in a creatively receptive environment. This is where people have open minds to different types of thinking and where the creative process is understood. Agencies and the creative people within the team need to be understood in terms of how they can add to the business and not just viewed as whacky because they bring their dog to work. Therefore it may be in your interests to ensure that appreciation of business–driven creativity is encouraged. The first port of call is the campaign team and then any other department who is involved in the approval process. Encourage yourself and colleagues to be open to creative influences. Some of my previous clients have employed the following ideas; they are suggestions that you and your team may be able to facilitate:

- Inform yourself and your colleagues on how an agency works behind the scenes.
- Circulate *Campaign*, *Creative Review*, *FT Creative Business*, etc.
- Show *Cannes Lions* or *Extreme* reels (for TV ad styles).
- Invite colleagues to attend award events.
- Visit local art exhibitions (particularly for photography).
- Have a pin board in the office with good and bad ads/direct mail, etc.

- Invest in a *Creative Whack Pack*® (Roger von Oech, 1992) (not a substitute for an agency but a host of suggestions for thinking laterally – available on Amazon).
- Put together 'Lunch and Learn' type talks about the company's marketing campaigns to share knowledge.
- Institute internal campaign brief awards.
- Institute 'Creative Inspiration' talks (e.g. get an architect to give a talk on the general creative process).
- Suggest to colleagues that they go on creative training courses (e.g. the ISBA *Appraising Creative Solutions* course).

PRESENTING CREATIVE EFFECTIVELY

Just think about some of the general presentations you have attended. Apparently there are 30 million PowerPoint® presentations delivered around the world every day! Some, no doubt, are enthralling while others will be absolute howlers. Some presenters can just infect you with passion while others have you racing for the door at the first possible opportunity. This is true of any type of presentation, so for a good creative presentation you need to let the principles of all good presentations guide you:

- Good preparation.
- Clarity (of purpose/of message).
- Connection with audience.
- Controlling the environment.

As you will probably need to re-present the agency's work to other departments, other colleagues or your boss, you should bear in mind the following when you do this:

1 Be happy that the concepts meet the brief and be confident that they will enrapture your colleagues.
2 Creative ideas do not 'sell' themselves. If it is an important presentation, take the time to rehearse it in front of a 'friendly' colleague and get

him/her to play devil's advocate, coming up with all the tricky questions. Some people will say that this is a luxury but, by doing this, you will potentially save yourself a lot of time.

3   Ideally set the meeting on your home turf. Psychologically this will be more advantageous for you; you are on familiar territory and you can stage-manage your environment to your taste.

4   Assess the importance of the meeting, and your capabilities of presenting winning concepts (do you need help from colleagues?). Understand it from your point of view, then mentally go around the other side of the table and assess it from the 'recipient's' perspective.

  – What is he/she expecting?
  – Who is he/she expecting?
  – What is the level of confidence in you, the agency and the creative product?
  – How important is the campaign?
  – Are there any other pressures?
  – What is the quality of finish expected of the presentation materials?

5   If you ask someone from the agency to present, make sure you are confident that he/she is aware of the specific business issues and internal sensitivities.

6   Decide what will be said, when and by whom.

7   When you arrive at the meeting, make sure that all the props are in place, that the projector/video and/or visual aids are in order, and that there is enough space to move around.

8   Assess your colleague's/boss's emotional state. Has he/she just been in a stressful previous meeting? Is he/she looking forward to the meeting?

9   Break the ice with introductions/small talk and teas and coffees to ensure that the atmosphere is receptive, not clinical.

10   Tell the colleague/boss what stages you are going to go through. Make sure he/she is happy with this and confirm timing.

11   The stages could be:

  – Recap on the brief/setting the scene.
  – Reminder of creative proposition/customer insight.

- Creative approach/idea.
- Concept presentation.
- Summing up (checklist of what the concept achieves).
- Fielding questions.
- Next steps.

TIP

I have always found it useful to ask for a written creative rationale to accompany the creative work – see Figures 5.4 and 5.5. This means that if you have to present it, you have something else tangible from the meeting that can prepare you for any questions.

12 You will need to create excitement about the concepts so that there is an atmosphere of anticipation. Yet, do not oversell.

13 Make sure you stage-manage your props and that each member of the meeting can see the materials. Do not focus only on the key decision-maker as it will rile the others. Also people do not always want to be the 'nodding dog' in the spotlight. However, maintain good eye contact and have the confidence to go through the different stages by telling a story – a story that is not only compelling but that you obviously and passionately believe in.

14 Before presenting, 'deconstruct' what you have to present. Learn it and explore it. Demonstrate your own understanding, passion and belief in what you are presenting.

15 Give your colleagues the space and time to get used to ideas, concepts, etc. If the concepts are tangible let them touch and feel them.

16 Walk through any clarifications, logistics/costs and issues (be prepared even if you know you do not have all the answers). Do not leave anything hanging.

17 At the end of the presentation, make sure that you leave them with concepts and info that they can share internally if that is necessary. At a basic level, these are photocopies/replicas. More comprehensively, this is a pack with a 'Questions and Answers' section and the reminder of the background and brief.

Partners **Andrews Aldridge**

Creative Rationale

Client:	Lloyds TSB
Project:	PhoneBank *Express* bill payment
Date:	21.03.04

Creative concept: 'Making it easier on your feet'

What are we attempting to do?

Our main communications task is to demonstrate to Lloyds TSB customers – who are already registered for PhoneBank *Express* (our automated phone-banking service) but are not using it – that they could be using it to their benefit.

This is a creative test that employs a more high profile route to make the message as impactful as possible and brings the benefits of the service to life.

What did we identify as the most powerful thing to say that could achieve this?

The quickest way to pay your bills is to pick up the phone.

What was the springboard for the creative idea?

The idea is rooted in the knowledge that using PhoneBank *Express* is an immediate service. There is no queuing and waiting. There is no need to go to a branch. When it comes to paying your bills, PhoneBank *Express* is the quick, free, easy and convenient way.

Definition of the creative idea

When you need to pay your bills, make sure that you are using PhoneBank *Express* which may be easier than having to go to a branch. In fact there is no waiting as there is no need to queue.
So you are 'making it easier on your feet' and choosing a very efficient way of paying your bills.

Executional elements that bring this to life

The outer envelope is a transparent wallet which allows you to see the line "Still walking to a branch to pay a bill?" Inside the pack, there are two shoe comfort liners. One of which emphasizes you may need them if you have to go to a branch. The other gives a better solution: "PhoneBank *Express* – a fast, free and easy way to pay your bills."

The whole pack is designed to be very impactful and bring the benefit of the service to life. Although it is humorous, it approaches the task in a down-to-earth way and shows how practical and efficient the PhoneBank *Express* service is.

Source: Reproduced by permission of Partners Andrews Aldridge/Lloyds TSB, 2004.

Figure 5.4 Example of creative rationale

Source: Reproduced by permission of Partners Andrews Aldridge and Lloyds TSB, 2004.

Figure 5.5   'Insoles' direct mail *'Still walking to a branch to pay a bill?'*

EXERCISES

1   Develop your own creative evaluation criteria.

2   Assess in the last three months how many concepts have been presented on brief.

3   Invite the creative director at your agency to talk about recent inspiring creative work.

SMOOTHING THE WAY FOR EFFECTIVE CAMPAIGNS

CHAPTER 6

SMOOTHING THE WAY FOR EFFECTIVE CAMPAIGNS

In this chapter you will learn about:

- Establishing project management systems.

- Approval procedures.

- Checking the legal aspects.

- Moving from concepts to campaign execution effectively.

- Managing problems with a creative concept.

We may operate in a creative environment but the day-to-day routine of the campaign development process is very much based on strong project management processes. In order to ensure that the creative product, in its transition from concept to execution, retains its market impact you and your agency need to have smooth project processes in place. There are a number of parties involved and it is your joint responsibility to keep the campaign on track in terms of outcome, time and budget. A spirit of partnership with your colleagues, your agency partners and other internal departments will allow you to develop and agree systems that will help you to deliver the desired outcome.

Yet, there will always be extenuating circumstances in campaigns, in fact issues and mistakes. Your boss does not like the concept although it is on brief and you think it will be a winner. An oversight by the production manager means that the print delivery will be five days late. Your legal team will not approve the headline without a 20-word caveat. There is not enough time to create the type of campaign necessary ('when is there ever?' I hear you cry). These are all familiar situations and yet it is how we legislate for them and react to them that will define our success.

ESTABLISHING PROJECT MANAGEMENT SYSTEMS

I think it is always worth regularly reviewing your campaign processes. Staff change, new team members work better in other circumstances, the nature of your campaigns vary and consequently your internal liaison can change. Also, systems can be improved; it is not that you are trying to find the nirvana of processes, it is more that you are trying to make them reflect everyday practice in order to match personal preferences and create efficiencies and ultimately campaign success. You do not have to employ management consultants to radically reform everything and formulate those horrendous flowcharts – you can study what you, your colleagues and agency do and fine-tune certain procedures and test new ways. In essence, let the following principles guide you:

- Clarity of goals and roles.
- A good project management team.
- Efficient project management procedures and administration.
- Effective communications.

Clarity of Goals and Roles

It seems obvious that in order to effect good project management, you need to be clear as to what you are trying to achieve and how each individual can contribute. However it is unusual, at the beginning of a project, that the combined team sits down and discloses their roles in relation to the goals. Some of this is assumed and at other times it happens on an *ad hoc* basis when colleagues want to understand the approval process or discover their contact in the legal department, or when agencies ask certain questions (e.g. "Do you want us to involve Steve, the planner? Who will be the lead agency on this campaign? Do you think we should talk to the media company?").

However, when there is a 'kick-off' meeting, the clarification of roles often becomes lost in the discussion of communication issues. The 'kick-off' meeting should, however, be an essential part of campaign planning and should be divided into two parts: (1) the discussion of the communications objectives and marketplace issues and (2) an exploration into how the team can work together to achieve the project management goals.

Project Management Team

You will be dealing with a number of internal functions, different agency/supplier contacts and with other members of the team in your department. Everyone at whatever level needs a sense of ownership. They must feel responsible for the success of the project, be committed to the team and make things happen. Consequently, if you are going to be working with a team in the long term, it is worth investing in making sure that the team dynamics work in your favour. I previously mentioned the use of psychometric assessments to allow the team to understand those with whom they are working. You should also consider team-building exercises, which break down a lot of the barriers, highlight the different individual styles and through 'fun and games' allow a team to gel. For a project leader, such assessment methods and bonding sessions may indicate any potential problems that you need to monitor.

COMMENT

There are companies where you can almost hear the internal groan when team-building exercises are mentioned. They envisage group hugs and balancing eggs on balloons; they think it is whacky for whackiness's sake. Others just cannot get enough of the playfulness but do not necessarily reap any of the rewards because they see it just as a bit of fun. Make sure that you match the style of team bonding to the culture and personalities of the group and also have it in a context that gives people permission to step out of the norm. Something I have found that works for both very 'straight' and outgoing groups in 'icebreaker' meetings is using a showreel of ads which are either dreadful, shocking, funny or just work really well, and getting them to talk about the ads in pairs and then in a group. You have to set it up in the right way and also link it to the task in hand (so also include a competitor ad/news item, for example). If you do not feel comfortable facilitating this, ask someone who is, and has the confidence of the group. Alternatively, if you want to link it more to the product, get that person to assume the role of a customer and give his/her reaction to a relevant product or communications material.

Project Management Procedures

Your company may have campaign procedures already established. You may be starting from scratch. Look at the key stages of *strategic planning, campaign briefing by the client, creative briefing in the agency, concept development, concept approval, concept execution, production/distribution* and *post-campaign evaluation* given in Chapter 2. Understand whether the procedure allows the best collaboration and output at each stage and then test any refinements once you have internal buy-in.

The questions that need to be asked are:

- Does everyone know their role?
- Who is involved at each stage?
- What milestones need to be passed at each stage?
- What information is necessary at each stage?
- Does everyone have an awareness of and conform to the approval procedures? (see below)
- Is everyone aware of budget and timing implications for each stage? (see Chapter 7)
- What are the quality checks?
- Are contingency plans in place?
- Is project administration established?

As already mentioned, project management is vastly improved by examining whether all team members know and buy into the overall process. The best way of making it clear is to document the process and share it with the team. When you do this, try to keep things simple and transparent.

Project Administration

This will differ according to the internal structure and the creative product involved but project administration can be categorized and recorded in electronic or hard files in such sections as:

- Internal department correspondence.
- Agency correspondence.
- Supplier/partner communications.
- Market background/research.
- Campaign briefing to agency.
- Campaign briefing internally/suppliers.
- Timing schedules/project plans.
- Cost estimates (internal).
- Cost estimates (agency/supplier/partner).
- Creative development.
- Production development.
- Legal issues.
- Purchase orders/invoicing.
- Final product.
- Issues/complaints log.

If kept up to date, project administration will help things to move more quickly and, because of the inherent transparency, allow colleagues to step in when there is sickness or annual leave.

TIP

All projects will not run as smoothly as they could do. That is just the unwritten law of project management. Nevertheless you can always improve your project management systems the next time around. Always have a 'wash-up' meeting session after the campaign. Use the Issues/Complaints log during the campaign to note any problems – a lot of the time issues are ignored at the end as people are just relieved that the campaign is over. Yet, such issues could potentially recur.

The 'wash up' session should be divided into parts: how the communications were developed; how effective they were; what issues arose in terms of campaign management; and how things can be improved. You should focus equally on the good areas as well as the issues. In fact, if it has been a big successful campaign, what about a celebratory thank-you drink? We all want to be thanked for our hard work and acknowledged for our contribution to the team's success.

Project Status Communications

In terms of regular communications, you should agree within the team what is necessary. You should hold regular status meetings to discuss progress of the campaigns and the agency should be tasked with issuing weekly/bi–weekly status reports and meeting contact reports.

The most important communications (in addition to those affecting the actual creative product) are any updates to the campaign costs and timings. Please encourage agencies/suppliers at all times to make you aware of any cost or timing implications.

Internal Communications

The best communication relationships are founded on mutual trust and confidence in each other's abilities. In running projects, good relationships can help you to achieve personal commitment, the potential of getting something extra, peace of mind and ultimately the desired project outcome.

Time needs to be invested in understanding the personalities and what motivates them. Build personal relationships and try to develop commonalities. Try to understand what pressures they are under, how they will react in a situation and what 'hot buttons' they respond to. For example, knowledge of a newly born baby will explain any tiredness or early departures in the afternoon and also give you a subject of conversation.

Although these considerations are pertinent to the wider team, a good deal of time and stress can be spared by facilitating the communications process with your internal colleagues in this way:

1   Exchange email addresses, mobile numbers and direct lines (and home numbers for emergencies).
2   Understand where your contact sits in the office so you can understand the context.
3   Ask your contact to visit your office environment.
4   Agree which communications should be handled by email, telephone or face-to-face, and which parties need to be included. (*NB*: Key stages should be done face-to-face.)
5   During busy campaigns, make sure that everyone is aware of everybody's daily whereabouts. Also, when timing schedules are discussed, identify any key conflicting dates (e.g. meetings, holidays).
6   Meetings should include:

    –   Statement of objectives including period of meeting.
    –   No distractions.
    –   Right people at right time.
    –   Summing up.
    –   Agreement of next actions/allocation of tasks.

7   Seek to resolve problems together.
8   Offer thanks and appreciation when due.
9   Be clear, fair and sensitive in any criticism.
10 Instill an understanding of the financial/deadline issues related to campaign.
11 State in advance what is required in terms of financial management/records.
12 Stipulate how and when any amendments to estimates and timing schedules should be communicated (e.g. verbally, then in writing within 24 hours).
13 When a campaign is moving quickly, flexibility needs to be employed. However always judge potential additional cost/time implications.

14   Try to have major discussions about costs face-to-face. Take emotion out of discussions.

15   As you move from step to step, ensure that the next actions and responsibilities are clear to colleagues.

APPROVAL PROCEDURES

At the beginning of the project, you and the rest of the team members need to be aware of the approval stages, who is involved and the protocol required to gain approval. The approval stages are quality control checks and indicators that show that those involved are happy to proceed.

The agency will have its own approval procedures. Therefore, make sure you are aware of them and that you understand their validity. Often, a good deal of frustration is caused at the client company because the artwork is waiting at the agency but the creative director has not yet seen it. In this case, this may happen because the creative director is responsible for the overall creative quality control and you are paying for such expertise to make sure you have the best product. The agency needs to build enough time into the schedule for this to happen without any frustration. And you need to make sure that the agency quality control is as informed as possible – ensuring that the agency has a good understanding of brand guidelines (design and tone of voice), legal/regulatory parameters and any other relevant considerations. You will then have your own approval checks. It is important that those who sign off the milestones know their scope and timeliness of approval. You do not want someone from the legal department commenting on the use of an image if it has nothing to do with any legal aspect. Similarly, you cannot have your boss commenting on the creative proposition when the brief was signed off two weeks ago and he/she is now looking at the concepts. You have to make it clear at the beginning of the project and be strong if it happens to the contrary at a later stage. Otherwise you will have to suffer the consequences.

That said, obviously, prices change, senior management may become stubborn and other departments may not be happy with certain aspects of campaigns. This is often the nature of organizations working at pace. If this affects the approval, you may have to concede that you need to change things, but it is imperative that you make all concerned aware of the time and cost implications of their decisions.

TIP

You often have a situation where your senior management take issue with a creative concept when in fact they have not seen the brief and 'bought into' the proposition. This can make your life very stressful. You need to try to curtail this by a pre-emptive strike (no suicide bombing just a bit of smart weaponry). You have to apprise the senior management of the agreed brief in advance. No way are they going to read through two pages of A4 but you may get them to look at a summary page (e.g. 1 page Powerpoint slide Proposition in bold 36pt, support and customer insight in plain 20pt). You need to communicate this to them or get your boss to do it. Otherwise you may have problems at concept sign-off.

CHECKING THE LEGAL ASPECTS

We read each week of campaigns contravening certain marketing standards guidelines. (The ASA alone dealt with over 14 000 complaints in 2003.) Or we know of the horror stories such as the 'Hoover flights promotion' which left a company exposed to great financial liability. Consequently, each campaign needs to be legally compliant, should not contravene your particular industry regulations and also subscribe to advertising/marketing guidelines. The legal side is a very complex area. Most importantly, your first port of call will be your in-house lawyer if you have one – and luckily there are also a number of bodies offering support and advice. Here are some pointers in dealing with legal matters concerning a campaign:

• All your communications should be legal, decent, honest and truthful.
• Your agency will only have a rudimentary understanding of all the legal issues surrounding the communications. Although they may know, for example, the Committee of Advertising (CAP) code very well, this will only be one set of regulatory guidelines which govern your communications. Your own lawyer should be the one guiding authority.
• Certain types of agencies are quite well versed in specific parts of the law governing communications (for example, direct marketing agencies

on Data Protection Act, sales promotion agencies on promotional terms and conditions).

- If you are a member of a marketing body such as the MCCA, the DMA, etc., you will have access to some of their legal services. If you are not a member, your agency may be (see Useful Information Sources in the Appendix).
- Your agency may have an in-house lawyer whom you may be able to consult.
- There are also some very good lawyers who specialize in marketing and promotional law (for example, Lawmark (www.lawmark.co.uk), who can give general advice or approve copy according to its legal standing).
- If you take external legal advice, you might want to clarify who is liable for that advice in the event of a problem. Ultimately, as the originator of customer communications, you are legally liable to your customers but you may have recourse having taken advice from a third party.
- It depends on the media you are using but the CAP code, downloadable from www.cap.org.uk, will give you a good understanding of its scope and the principles applying to areas such as competitive comparisons, testimonials, guarantees, etc. The ASA (Advertising Standards Authority), as well as providing regulation, has an e-newsletter to keep people informed of adjudications (requestable from www.asa.org.uk).
- Ofcom was set up to further the interests of consumers with regard to broadcast and telephone media and regulate accordingly. Make sure you are aware of the codes and policies, which can be viewed at www.ofcom.org.uk. As of November 2004, the ASA is now involved in a collaboration with Ofcom to monitor standards on radio and TV.

TIP

Working with your legal department will require all your diplomatic skills. Quite rightly they are very cautious and do not want to expose your company to any legal or regulatory liability. Sometimes the lawyer ends up being the copywriter because you and the agency are given the exact wording (e.g. an addition to the headline which makes things very long and unwieldy) rather than the scope to revisit the headline according to the specific issue. If this is the case, try to ask your lawyer for the freedom to reword the copy in the style of the overall text rather than taking the legal wording variation. What also worked with one of my financial clients was that our copywriter and the legal contact actually spoke directly on a regular basis to avoid such situations.

MOVING FROM CONCEPTS TO CAMPAIGN EXECUTION EFFECTIVELY

It is very difficult to give a full overview in this area when the media in different situations can be so diverse, but it has been recognized in all disciplines that concept development and production/distribution of the finished article can be fraught with miscommunication and errors on both sides. Therefore ensure that you have robust quality control checks in place. On a general level, consider the following as you move through the process:

1   Anyone on your side who will have a say on the creative concept approval needs also to approve the creative brief.
2   Confirm with the agency what level of finish the creative work will have at the presentation stage.
3   Determine whether the agency has a policy of presenting one or more concepts.
4   Request supplementary items that will help you to present the concepts on further internally (e.g. written creative rationale, extra visuals/tapes, pdfs, etc.).
5   Assess legal/regulatory issues before approval.
6   Assess how concepts fit in with overall brand positioning (will anyone take issue with this?).
7   Assess production feasibility/costs/timings before final approval.
8   Make final approval dependent on the presentation of updated agency timing schedules/cost estimates.
9   Make sure you have the authority to give final approval.
10 Consider internal systems/success measurement implications.
11 Once concepts are approved, stay close to concept execution and production.
12 Make sure you understand how the creative treatment is going to be developed (photography style, choice of director, etc.). Be comfortable with the agency recommendation.

13   Request photographers' books, director reels or paper samples to under-stand any agency recommendation.

14   Attend photographic shoots where possible.

15   Decide the most efficient copy sign-off route.

16   Identify who are the 'project managers' at the agency and get them to keep you informed on an ongoing basis.

17   Test production/execution where possible (e.g. press runs, paper stock, etc.).

18   Pre-order samples/tapes/run-outs for internal communications and your records.

19   Make sure you are the first to see the final product.

COMMENT

There can be a little tension over the number of concepts that are created for the presentation meeting. It is worth understanding the policy of the agency on this point. Some will only ever present one, some will present one with discarded alternatives to show the progression of thinking, and others will present two or three with an agency recommendation. Certain clients feel more comfortable with seeing a few concepts and are disappointed with just seeing one treatment. If you always need to see three, you will need to agree that with the agency as there are time and cost implications for such consistent extra work. However, you might agree that, mostly, you would like to see two but if the brief does not allow or warrant more than one, you will be happy with that. This builds in flexibility and could mean that you see three concepts on occasions. What you really want to avoid is one treatment being added just to make up the numbers and to sway your choice to the frontrunner.

If you see more than one concept, you also have to be disciplined not to take an element of Concept 1, an element of Concept 2 and something from Concept 3 and ask the agency to come back with a new concept based on your cocktail. This flies in the face of creating single-minded communications.

MANAGING PROBLEMS WITH A CREATIVE CONCEPT

Whether on the agency or the client side, we often have ridiculous deadlines, work with some people who are very good at getting what they want and with other people who have problems expressing themselves, and ultimately we are judged on how we work with all these factors to achieve delivery.

We need to admit to ourselves that this is the business we are in. These are not extraordinary circumstances; this is the norm as marketers. We are by definition problem-solvers and by working as agencies and clients we are being paid to find solutions to problems at all points of campaign development.

You will often get a situation where a colleague or department will not accept a concept. The reason has to lie within one of four areas: the concept itself; the presenting of the concept; the receipt of the concept by the colleague; and your relationship with the colleague.

You can influence the presentation and receipt of the concept along the way by involving the colleague in the process (at creative brief approval or campaign briefing), talking through the general creative approaches in advance of the meeting and presenting alternative concepts as this helps them to understand how you have formulated the recommended approach.

Yet if you analyse things more closely, sometimes something else is awry. The problem often lies outside the concept but more in the relationship between you and the colleague(s) and the corresponding management of expectations. I would therefore recommend focusing on the preparation before a problem arises. You will have more chance of getting a successful result than reversing a *fait accompli*. (Otherwise you will end up deciding the outcome on whose boss is the bigger.)

So what do you do when the agency has come up with a brilliant concept and it is not welcomed because it is too bold or badly timed? Unfortunately there is no instant panacea for this situation but you may wish to act in this way:

1   Approach the discussion in an open frame of mind. Put the colleague at ease.
2   Make the colleague feel that he/she is being listened to.
3   Check whether the colleague has understood the concept.
4   Check whether he/she is not happy with the core idea or the execution.
5   Assess immovability – probe issues and see whether the problems can be resolved with minor adaptations.
6   Discuss what is on your colleague's mind and talk in the abstract about alternative approaches.

7   Seek to understand whether this is the last port of call (or if it can be presented to the colleague's boss or you can engage your boss to act as a persuader).

8   Be careful not to isolate the colleague by presenting 'over his/her head' to others.

9   If he/she is immovable, get the colleague to articulate again in an email what the issues are.

10   Rebrief the agency team.

COMMENT

This can be one of those major stress points in campaign development because of extra time implications. However, you need to rise above the personal stress and consequently inspire the agency team to resolve the situation and create a new solution. This is possible with practicable feedback about the concepts. Make sure that you are given workable feedback and that you also supply thoughts on other potential approaches and identify any blind-alleys. Remember also to ask the agency if there are any cost and timing implications from this setback.

Talking to the Agency about Problems with a Concept

If you understand the issues with the concept and you exercise clarity in your explanations, this can be a straightforward exercise. Therefore you may want to spend a little time in formulating your response to the agency. If it is quite important, you may wish to choose some or all of the following options:

- Hold a face-to-face meeting at the agency.
- Request a meeting with the relevant creative team/creative head to discuss things personally.
- Formulate feedback in writing in advance.
- Assess whether feedback is actionable (i.e. the agency would know how to resolve the issue).

- Understand whether it is a minor amendment or a restart (do not disguise one as the other) and assess the cost and time implications.
- If it is just because you do not like it, say so but say why and how you do not like it.

These are always sensitive conversations where you have to use your diplomacy. You have to dismantle the agency's belief that a winning concept has been presented, and get the agency to identify the elements of the concept that are correctly in place. You must also ask the agency to create a new concept with the same vigour that was used to create the first one.

Using the principles of feedback stated in Chapter 5, a conversation could go like this:

> Mike, I wanted to talk to you about the press ad for this new book we are publishing. Do you have time to talk about it? As you know, considering its importance to the author, I have shown it to everyone involved here and there were some very positive comments coming out. They liked the way your team had used the insight about the target group not having a lot of time for masses of business books, they liked that the call to action was integrated into the headline and you have been succinct – the way we like it. Yet there are still reservations about the overall thought: 'Time is running out. Make the call. Enlightenment or ignorance?' juxtaposed against an image of a telephone in the shape of an egg timer next to the book. There is a feeling that the headline crystallizes the issue into a too 'black and white' context and is a little patronizing. I also do not feel that it really reflects the aspiration we injected into the proposition. Overall, although people liked the focused thinking, they did not feel comfortable with the tone and extreme distillation of the thought. They felt the 'take or leave it' approach would turn off the majority of the readers.
>
> Therefore I am sorry to say that we need to look at another concept. But I am keen to retain the customer insight and the clever succinctness of message. I am happy to come in and talk to the team and discuss their views on how we move forward. I think they have already unearthed an interesting approach which *The Economist* uses very well. I don't think it will take long to work out our way forward. Maybe you could debrief the team and I will come into the agency tomorrow to see them and discuss timings. In the meantime, I will put this in an email to you.

COMMENT

If you are in a genuine partnership with your agency, you will both come to a mutually satisfactory solution to any problem. Make sure, in your hurry to get things back on track, that you do not steamroller over the platform of goodwill you have built up. Agencies, if they are responsible partners, will work with you both to resolve the situation and to claim back some of the lost time.

EXERCISES

1 Identify where the approval bottlenecks are internally.

2 Understand where you spend your time in the campaign development process.

3 Ask your colleagues for their views on where improvements could be made in the process.

TAKING CARE
OF THE FINANCES
OF THE RELATIONSHIP

CHAPTER 7

TAKING CARE OF THE FINANCES
OF THE RELATIONSHIP

In this chapter you will learn about:

- Different agency remuneration structures.

- Working with procurement.

- Contract or no contract?

- Setting a budget.

- How an agency works in terms of finances.

Satisfaction with the financial aspect of the relationship is a good barometer of whether both sides are happy with the relationship overall. Get this right and you can sleep at night. This is the bedrock of any client–agency partnership and the area where friction can occur if the framework is not established correctly at the beginning. There are a number of ways an agency can be remunerated for its work and it is worth exploring these to determine what is best for you and your agency. In addition, you will need to decide if the relationship warrants a legally binding contract and how other departments such as purchasing or procurement can help you to develop the partnership and gain any efficiencies. Moreover, if you are working with the agency on a day-to-day project basis and dealing with campaign costs and invoicing, it will be invaluable to understand how an agency structures its finances.

DIFFERENT AGENCY REMUNERATION STRUCTURES

If agencies live and die by their creation of ideas, how much does an idea cost and what and who is involved in the cost aspect of the idea? And how much is a great idea worth compared to a mediocre one? Should it be related to the overall media or production costs? These are the dilemmas with which the industry has struggled as financial relationships have developed. Similarly, although a digital agency delivers a creative product as much as an events management company, the time and production elements are quite different.

This has all led to different remuneration models employed between clients and agencies. There are four basic models with accompanying hybrids:

- Commission.
- Phased fee.
- Project fee.
- Payment by results.

Commission

This is where the agency charges a percentage on top of the production or media associated with a campaign. This method is rooted in the evolution of advertising agencies and gave rise to the terms 'above the line' and 'below the line'. Originally, this was the basis on which all agencies charged: retaining the standard media commission or adding 17.65% to the net media costs (i.e. the commission being 15% of the gross cost) to cover their time. The media owners rebated the commission solely to the agencies. Later, as certain clients developed different media relationships and as media buying became a separate entity, the commission was shared among the creative agency, the media agency and the client. What defined an agency, therefore, was the 'line' where the commission was drawn. So, historically, 'above the line' agencies were those who produced creative work that would be broadcast through commission-associated media (then predominantly posters, press and TV) while 'below the line' activity (then mainly direct mail and sales promotion materials) was commission-free – for example, there was no commission when using someone's letterbox to spread your marketing message. Things have changed radically now, but interestingly the terms linger. Nevertheless, the commission basis is still with us and has been extended to other external costs.

What people like about a commission basis is that it is simple. If you have a budget of €200 000, you and the agency know that the agency will get €20 000 if the commission is 10% of the gross. However it is no reflection of the agency time involved. This is critical for the agency if the total budget is relatively small for the task in hand and critical for the client if the budget is large for a rudimentary project (in fact you could argue that it encourages the agency to spend more). For example, a sales promotion agency working on a percentage of the production placed will make a loss if it is asked to source 10 individually engraved iPods but may make excessive profit if it sources two million address books which it has sourced before. An agency can only function profitably if it is engaged mainly in larger activity and its creative and project management time is covered. In order to avoid excessive profits, sliding scales of commission have been introduced and/or the commission basis is used in conjunction with other forms of remuneration.

Phased Fee

As in any service industry, an agency has only its time to sell. This time may be translated into strategic thinking, creative work or digital programming, but ultimately what will keep the agency in business is how it manages its staff time. Consequently, time-based remuneration is the emerging method of choice for the agency world. On the client side, it is finding favour because it is accountable and comparable to other service providers.

The phased fee method is one way in which time-based remuneration can be used. In its calculation, there is a resource planning stage, a phased monthly fee, and the time spent on campaigns is monitored to match against the 'retainer' fee.

Typically the client and the agency would sit down and discuss a period of activity, such as a year's campaigns, and decide the agency personnel that will be needed to plan, create and execute the activity. For example, the client activity may mean that 50% of a Senior Planner is needed along with 100% of a creative team and 75% of an Account Director and Account Manager. The agency will have a rate card with hourly rates for each member of staff and, subsequently, a total budget can be arrived at for the year. The total fee budget is then divided into monthly phased amounts. At regular periods, client and agency will make sure that the monthly fee reflects the reality of agency involvement.

There are many variants of this, including those where only certain personnel are retained (e.g. the account team) but where creative resource is paid for separately or where there are no diverse hourly rates but just an agreed average agency rate. Whatever the form, the phased fee has the advantage of predictable cashflow on both sides and it secures the client-specific people in the agency who can work on the business, ensuring consistency and increased learning. It also means that projects can be initiated without individual paperwork being needed for each project, and that an agency can move without a purchase order each time. Although this method is widespread there is a feeling on the client side that agencies can become inefficient and that a retained service is no guarantee of quality of work. My belief is that the lack of the latter is not a function of retained services and there are enough ways to monitor efficiency (through time analysis and external benchmarking) and quality of work can be maintained by other aspects of the partnership (regular client satisfaction assessments, creative reviews and results monitoring).

TIP

When a relationship starts to break down, the reason often expressed is lack of *Value for Money*. This is normally a symptom rather than a cause, but to ensure that this perception does not creep into your relationship, it is important that you are happy with your time calculations at the beginning of negotiations and consistently through the partnership. Otherwise it can colour your judgement in other areas – strategic recommendations from the agency, creative work and ultimately your view of the campaign results. First of all, make sure that you are comfortable with the agency hourly rates. (ISBA members have access to rate card guidelines. If you are not a member, your trade organization may provide a similar service, or one of the third-party organizations mentioned in Chapter 3 may be able to help you.) Once a fee has been agreed, determine how the agency is going to report on its time analysis and how you may adjust the fee later to reflect reality. And make sure you diarize meetings so that the fee is regularly monitored.

In addition, when assessing the hourly rates, understand how these are calculated and the margins on which they are based. For example, an agency may be working on a ratio of Earnings Before Interest and Tax (EBIT) against total operating income of between 15% and 20%. If you are a major client you may be able to have a dialogue to see whether there is any flexibility on this if you guarantee a certain amount of income.

Project Fee

This is another time-based method and is where the agency charges solely for the project in hand. It can be calculated from a pre-agreed menu of project fees or estimated before the project starts. The same principles of benchmarking and monitoring are valid here. It is popular with clients who award projects on an *ad hoc* basis or have a roster of agencies for different tasks.

Payment by Results

This results-oriented remuneration basis tends to be in addition to another method, as opposed to stand-alone. The benchmarks can be the business results, the agency service, the marketing communications created or a combination of the three. It is gaining popularity as it incentivizes the agency to deliver accountable results and binds the agency into the wider marketing team (particularly if the business results are being measured). The crux is how the results can be measured and whether they can be directly attributable to one agency's activity. In addition, it is also how great the performance-related element is in the context of the remuneration, and this depends on the nature of the activity and the speculative attitude of both parties.

Whichever form it takes, it is worth mentioning that a cap should be placed on any PBR agreement in order to avoid the effects of any market anomalies.

The IPA and ISBA have issued some guidelines which will help anyone thinking about PBR. They suggest considering the following in advance:

1   **Context.** PBR should be considered within the context of the overall client–agency relationship and the whole remuneration agreement. Typically PBR is an enhancement to existing remuneration, payable on the achievement of mutually agreed targets for enhanced advertiser satisfaction. PBR is not in itself a cure for significant relationship problems or an inequitable remuneration agreement.
2   **Win–win.** The PBR scheme should be mutually beneficial (for both client and agency). Agencies are more predisposed to PBR generally if costs are covered and there is opportunity to earn a greater reward. Advertisers are predisposed to PBR if they are not paying more for the expected level of agency service and performance. The goal is to devise a win-win situation – higher profits for agencies and more measurable satisfaction for clients.
3   **Objectives.** Both agency and client should be clear on their objectives for embracing PBR. Although the primary objective is direct improvement in performance, a good scheme can also have partnership benefits as agency and client are more open, accountable and motivated. A PBR scheme can focus thinking on clarity of roles and objectives, improve efficiency and be an agent for organizational change.
4   **Difficulties.** PBR is not without potential difficulties and drawbacks. Discussions on the structure of the scheme and measures to be employed may be protracted in the search to achieve both simplicity and fairness. If ill-conceived the PBR scheme may result in focusing on narrow and short-term objectives at the expense of brand building. PBR may not be suitable, possible or desirable for a variety of reasons including the relevance of measures to the task, the availability of data and the flexibility of the marketing budget. However, discussions on PBR will likely be useful even if it is not adopted.

Source: Finding an Agency – Joint industry guidelines reproduced by permission of DMA, IPA, ISBA, MCCA and the PRCA (2004). More discussion of PBR is contained in Section 25. Fully downloadable from each of the trade bodies' websites.

WORKING WITH PROCUREMENT

If you have a department such as procurement, purchasing or 'agency/supplier management' in your organization, there is an opportunity to join forces with them to make your agency relationship more effective. This really depends on procurement's remit and how departments are structured to effect cooperation.

More and more companies are investing in having procurement/purchasing specializing in marketing services and a few organizations such as Lloyds TSB have departments responsible for the management of the relationship with agencies and suppliers. They can add value in areas such as:

- Agency/supplier landscape knowledge.
- Evaluation and selection of agencies/suppliers.
- Dialogue with agency/supplier finance departments.
- Management of the campaign development process.
- Efficient procurement of marketing materials.
- Contract/remuneration negotiation.
- Internal arbitration.
- Ongoing agency benchmarking.
- Management of a roster.
- Connection to the other parts of the business.

Those marketers who have worked with procurement for some time value their different viewpoint and appreciate the difference of approach in helping to make the agency relationship more effective. At one end of the spectrum, procurement can reduce the print costs significantly by consolidating suppliers. At the other end, the same department can also be managing the agency evaluation process in tandem with the marketing department, using the same rigour that they use to evaluate their lawyers or management consultants.

In more and more companies, procurement and marketing departments are working more closely together. They have spent time getting to know each other's language and agendas. They have established a regular dialogue with several consequences. Now that procurement experts have understood that they need to take a different approach to marketing procurement, their focus is more on *value-enhancement* rather than just cost savings. Marketing, with a better understanding of procurement, is starting to involve them at an earlier stage – in agency selection, contract negotiations and campaign budgeting.

Initially, agencies were suspicious of the involvement of procurement/purchasing in their relationship with marketing clients. At times, they were afraid (sometimes quite justifiably) that creative work was being judged in the same light as office equipment, but now with better knowledge on both sides and a stronger dialogue between the internal departments, things are changing. In fact, certain agency groups are employing their own purchasing personnel in order to be able to understand the procurement perspective and allow a more balanced dialogue to occur.

Once again ISBA has done some work in this area and assembled 35 experienced marketing procurement professionals from major blue-chip companies to give their views on what they thought helped to manage the relationship with their communications agencies: The following were their tips:

1   Visible support from the marketing hierarchy for the procurement function helps to establish the seriousness of the company's commitment to purchasing's involvement in the agency relationship and presents a united front to the agency – sometimes agencies try to marginalize procurement so this unity of support is vital.
2   Talk the agency's language and understand their core activities and skills.
3   Be willing to invest time to understand how the agency operates and gain an understanding of their issues and pressure points.
4   Consider a secondment into the agency so procurement can understand first hand the agency's core skills and processes and working practices.
5   The agency needs to be clear on the role of procurement so communication of scope of role, goals and objectives are essential – think about presenting formally to your agency team – what is procurement all about; what do we want from our agencies; what is procurement's role; how does procurement work with marketing; how can procurement help enhance the relationship, etc.?
6   Listen to the agency and involve them in improving 'best practice' at the client end.
7   Procurement should act as the internal guardian of the client/agency relationship – implementing formal 360 degree relationship evaluations, ensuring invoices get paid on time, mediating on disputes, encouraging effectiveness modelling, ensuring proper process for managing pitches, encouraging 'best practice' process internally, e.g. briefing. Therefore they can act as a contact point outside the day-to-day relationship with marketing for agency personnel if there are issues that need addressing.
8   Ensure that there is a balance between the needs of the organization and needs of the agencies – create win–win situations.
9   Procurement should not get in the way of the agency relationship with marketing but should act as another prong to the relationship between the business and the agency.
10 Be fair – investigate what your company could do differently, rather than just pushing the agency to change process and think of the agency as a business partner.
11 Share purchasing tools and techniques with the agency to enhance their ability to manage your company's communications investment more effectively and efficiently, e.g. offer the agency your company travel deals; look at optimum sourcing of print; encourage the agency to negotiate deals with production houses, etc.

12   Procurement should be honest and open as far as is sensible with the agency and be seen as a conduit or filter through which relations can be enhanced and productivity increased.

13   Procurement should provide objectivity and deal in facts.

14   Procurement should try and understand agency cost drivers and listen to agency suggestions for reducing costs, in terms of simplifying the briefing process, over servicing, re-work, etc. Recognize that client behaviour can often produce inefficiencies and impact the way in which agencies work and charge.

15   Forming a good working relationship with the agency finance director or commercial director, working together to understand what drives their costs and where their margin is made enables more effective relationships and negotiations.

16   Ensure procurement is involved in review meetings with the agency.

17   Always be prepared to ask questions of the agency to ensure full understanding.

18   Procurement needs to demonstrate that by being involved in the relationship it can actually help increase agency revenue, e.g. by identifying other opportunities around their group, either brands or companies, agreeing long-term contracts allowing the agency to secure revenue stream, helping agencies to reduce their internal costs.

Source: 'Top tips' for procurement relationships with agencies (2004). Reproduced by permission of ISBA. Available for members on request at www.isba.org.uk.

CONTRACT OR NO CONTRACT?

The above may sound like a funny question in the cold light of day but it is amazing how many longstanding, very professional client–agency relationships do not have contracts. This may be because it is forgotten in the 'honeymoon period' or the negotiations were abandoned out of boredom, frustration or deadlock. On one account I know of, it took three years for a contract to be agreed as the 'back and forth' between agency and client (and between the agency's lawyers and client's lawyers) was extended because it was a contract for a roster of agencies.

So the answer to the above is a simple 'yes' but it should be accompanied by the advice to seal the contract within two weeks of selection and be disciplined about it. In fact I was involved in negotiations of a recent account win where the procurement department set a three-day deadline and would not announce the selection publicly until the contract had been agreed in principle. That definitely focused the conversations.

The key areas that need to be confirmed are (1) remuneration structure, (2) copyright and (3) notice-period as it is in both parties' interests to have these settled before any problems occur. In addition, service level agreements, confidentiality, scope of work, process and legal recourse will also need to be stipulated. There are a number of model contracts available through ISBA, IPA and other trade bodies. The model for direct marketing and sales promotion agencies can be viewed at www.mcca.org.uk.

SETTING A BUDGET

If you are planning the overall communications budget for the first time, it can be an intimidating process. Where do you start? What is the total you set? How do you know to weight the budget towards advertising, direct marketing or PR, etc.?

The most common practices of setting an overall budget are:

1   Matching the objectives with the tasks needed to achieve them.
2   Maintaining last year's levels.
3   A percentage of forecast sales.
4   Affordability.
5   A percentage of last year's sales.
6   Fixed cost per unit of sales.
7   Matching competitive spend.

These are not mutually exclusive and in reality a preferred method is used and tempered with others to sanity-check the amount. In an ideal world, budgets would be set based solely on Method 1 but I know that Method 4 will always come into play and Method 3 is probably the commonly preferred lead approach.

In terms of deciding how to allocate budget according to marketing discipline, you will probably need to start with the basics of understanding the communications objectives. If you need to achieve increased awareness as a basis for sales, then perhaps advertising and PR need to be up-weighted. If your audience is only online, a heavy web allocation will be considered. What I would suggest is that you thrash out these issues with colleagues, your media agency and any other agency partners in a pre-budget meeting and then allow this to inform your allocations. You may also ask your media company if it is experienced in econometric modelling, computer-generated models that identify the channel/medium from which specific sales, enquiries, awareness, etc., are coming. At present, this concept is still at the 'holy grail' stage for some marketers as it really depends on them accessing all pertinent internal and market information to build a robust model (which is always going to be difficult). Then again, you may be lucky and have a totally accountable marketing operation which can make use of such modelling to inform your budget decisions.

HOW AN AGENCY WORKS IN TERMS OF FINANCES

If you are working with an agency that acts as your partner and agent, you need to be comfortable with how the agency manages both your campaign costs and its own finances. The more transparency there is, the more trust will develop. It is therefore worth understanding the finances at the various stages:

- Campaign budgeting.
- Issuing an accurate campaign estimate.
- Invoicing.
- Final reconciliations.

COMMENT

I hate to introduce a note of negativity here, but it seems that a small number of clients have a cynical perception that agencies are somehow ripping clients off. I believe this is a hangover from the 1980s when there were some dodgy dealings. Maybe it is because some agency people still come over as a little too slick for their own good and give the impression that they are hiding something. Otherwise, it could be because there can be vast differences between agencies and their hourly rates. Whatever the reason for this perception, my experience is that agencies nowadays earn their dollar honestly but it is true that their time comes at a premium. Maybe agency people should just settle into the fact that they are up there with lawyers as one of the professional services' 'bogeymen'. Nevertheless, for your part you should feel very comfortable with the agency financial processes and display trust during the campaign development. Therefore take time at the beginning of the relationship to iron out any of your questions. If you are new to this side of things, enlist a colleague to help you.

To highlight what you will encounter financially in the campaign process, I will name each stage showing, firstly, the guiding principles that I recommend to any account handler. You may wish to assess whether your agency is performing in these areas:

1 **Efficient administration.**   Your account handler needs to be highly disciplined and to record all costs sent to you and received from internal departments/third-party suppliers. You should ask at some point to see how this is done. This will help you to know how the process works when you are in the thick of campaign development.

2 **Comprehensive overview.**   A good campaign finance manager will always have 'helicopter vision', in other words the ability to see things from some distance and understand the big picture. When it comes to costs, it is necessary to see how individual elements are interdependent, what cost implications (such as amendments) certain decisions have and whether the overall budget total is being jeopardized. In a campaign, do not allow tight timings to railroad your account handler into not being on top of the finances. For example, when it comes to emergency retouching of photography, make sure the agency gives you a rough cost estimate in advance or set a budget limit yourself. You may be thinking only that the shots need amending in time for the print deadline, but another major consideration is that the accelerated retouching may come at a premium price and break the budget.

3 **Transparency.**   You do not need to see every invoice, but as a client I would write into your contract agreement that you have the right to audit campaign costs. It keeps the agency team disciplined and on their toes. Then every so often, I would ask for the final campaign reconciliation to include original invoices.

4 **Expectation management.**   No one wants to receive any nasty shocks about costs over-running. I think it is your joint responsibility to have

an open dialogue about costs and not allow time pressures to put a metaphorical gun against your heads over costs. As I have said before, if you feel less experienced in this area, make sure that you talk cost issues with a colleague for advice or make it clear to the account director that you want to be informed of any additional cost implication as the campaign evolves.

Campaign Budgeting

Campaign budgeting is the process of defining the total part of money needed to execute a campaign and breaking the total amount into the various campaign cost elements (see Figure 7.1). You may be qualified to do this without the agency's help. However, involving the agency at this early stage encourages its emotional buy-in, confirms joint estimation of costs and allows the agency to alert you to any costs you may have forgotten. If you ask the agency to formulate the campaign budget, make sure you provide as much information as possible to enable the agency to give you an accurate costing:

- What is the total budget?
- What are the business and sales objectives?
- What are the communications objectives and measures?
- Do you have an understanding of audience quantities?
- Is there an allowable market cost per sale/enquiry?
- Have there been campaigns similar to this?
- What media do you intend to use?
- What needs to be included (call centre responses, fulfilment, etc.)?

COMMENT

Agencies are often accused of not being as careful with the clients' money as they could be. I have a theory that this can sometimes be inadvertently encouraged at the outset at the campaign budgeting stage. Clients often ask agencies to come up with campaign budgets but say they do not have a formal budget. The agency then comes back with an excessive budget, which forces you to think more about the parameters and nominate a figure. My theory is that this process engenders

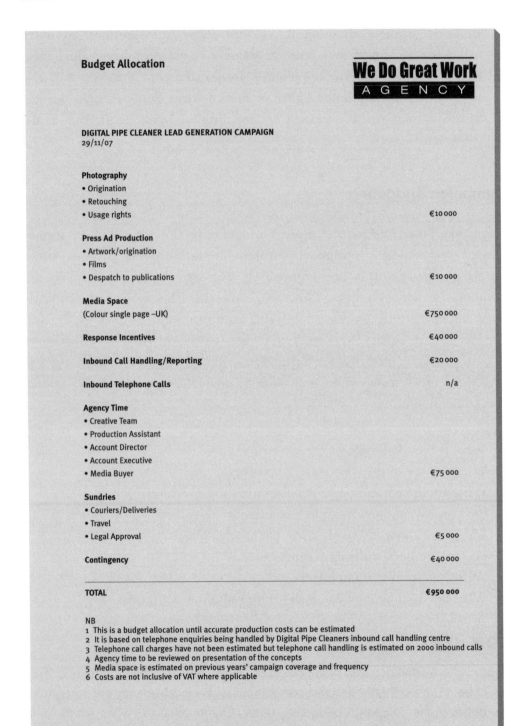

Budget Allocation

We Do Great Work
A G E N C Y

DIGITAL PIPE CLEANER LEAD GENERATION CAMPAIGN
29/11/07

Photography
• Origination
• Retouching
• Usage rights   €10 000

Press Ad Production
• Artwork/origination
• Films
• Despatch to publications   €10 000

Media Space
(Colour single page –UK)   €750 000

Response Incentives   €40 000

Inbound Call Handling/Reporting   €20 000

Inbound Telephone Calls   n/a

Agency Time
• Creative Team
• Production Assistant
• Account Director
• Account Executive
• Media Buyer   €75 000

Sundries
• Couriers/Deliveries
• Travel
• Legal Approval   €5 000

Contingency   €40 000

TOTAL   €950 000

NB
1 This is a budget allocation until accurate production costs can be estimated
2 It is based on telephone enquiries being handled by Digital Pipe Cleaners inbound call handling centre
3 Telephone call charges have not been estimated but telephone call handling is estimated on 2000 inbound calls
4 Agency time to be reviewed on presentation of the concepts
5 Media space is estimated on previous years' campaign coverage and frequency
6 Costs are not inclusive of VAT where applicable

Figure 7.1   Sample campaign budget allocation

in an agency a disrespect for the finances of the campaign. Therefore, even if you do not have a fixed budget in mind, give the agency the basic info as above to enable the process to start on a more realistic basis.

Issuing an Accurate Campaign Estimate

An estimate by the agency is a more accurate summary of potential campaign costs than a budget (see Figure 7.2). It can be presented in parts or in one estimate, as a result of the campaign brief in anticipation of the creative campaign.

In dealing with estimates from the agency think about the following:

- Encourage agencies to use a standard template so that the format becomes familiar to you. Also Excel spreadsheets reduce the risk of adding up inaccuracies.
- Ideally ask your agency to take you though the budget face-to-face to reduce the risk of misinterpretation.
- Have the option to ask for back-up of third-party estimates to understand cost elements in detail.
- Clarify whether VAT is included or not.
- Compare the estimate to your campaign budget.
- Has the agency added in all the possible costs – legal, promotion insurance, travel/couriers, initial quality tests, contingency (always factor this in for unknowns)?

TIP

Costs are always a sensitive area for both agencies and their clients. You can easily spend an excessive amount of time querying costs. Therefore you should initially work with your agency to standardize cost elements and procedures in order to reduce that time. Ideally you should agree, in advance, hourly rates and standard campaign fees (this will save you a huge amount of time). Plus confirm estimate, purchase order and invoicing procedures. For example, you may wish to agree a standard charge for developing a press ad or to institute a procedure whereby the agency has to have received three competitive quotes for its print.

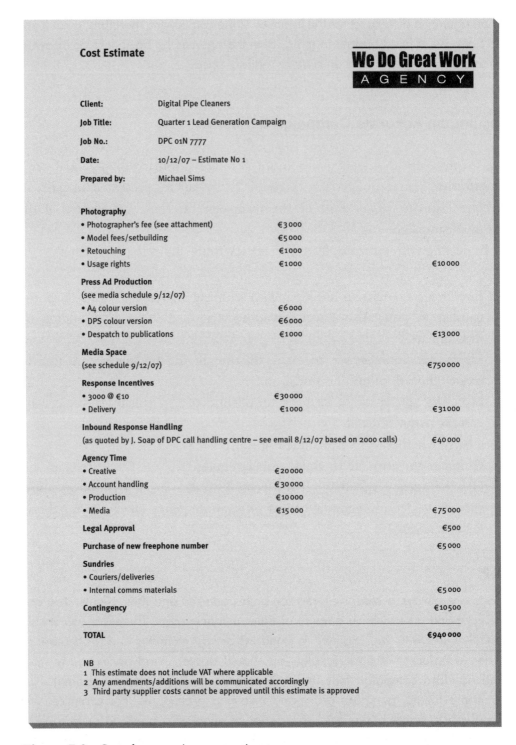

Figure 7.2 Sample campaign cost estimate

COMMENT

Remember that once you sign these costs off, the agency is acting on your behalf. Therefore you need to be comfortable with these costs and also to establish what freedom the agency has in deviating from the costs without informing you. Also bear in mind that you may need to pay certain costs (e.g. photographers' fees) in advance of the work.

Invoicing

If you are new to agency campaign finances, people will refer to what sounds like a 'whip' and you will think instinctively that the agency is involved in some kinky 'fun and games'. In fact this is the financial Work In Progress report, which helps the agency to monitor campaign costs. It includes:

- The actual costs that have been allocated to the campaign.
- The purchase orders that have been raised to third-party suppliers for future incoming costs.
- The items that have been invoiced against the costs.
- The items that have been billed in advance of expected costs.

An example of an agency WIP report is shown in Figure 7.3.

The WIP report will be the basis of the invoicing that is sent to you. You do not need to see this, but ask out of interest to see this system to reassure yourself of the agency's processes and mechanisms to monitor and reconcile campaign costs.

In terms of invoicing, bear in mind the following:

- You may need to raise purchase orders so that agency invoicing can take place. In certain agreements, agencies do not initiate a campaign until the PO has been raised. Do not allow a campaign to be stalled through inefficient administration.
- Invoicing for one campaign may come in at different stages. Agree up front what the phasing should be.
- Be prepared to pay certain invoices in advance of the work. This is because monies are needed to pay certain suppliers in advance of their work.

Job Overview

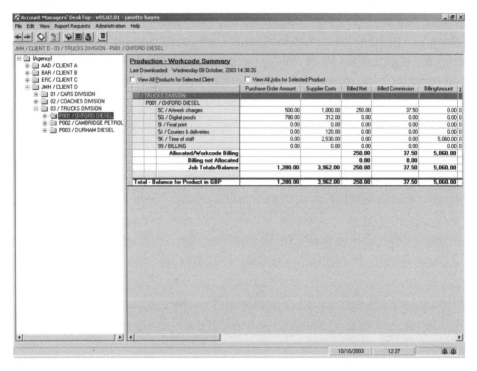

Job Detail

Workcode Details – JMH / 03 / P001   [10 October, 2003 11:10]

		Reference	Order No.	O/S Orders	Net Amount	Net Billed	Bill No.	Bill Date	Narrative
5C / Artwork charges									
	SVAGBP / SUPPLIER 2								
	02/09/2003	003121	003182	0.00	250.00	250.00	109003	01/10/2003	1ST DRAFT ARTWORK
	12/09/2003	998762	DUMMY	0.00	750.00	0.00			
	24/09/2003		003183	500.00	0.00	0.00			
	Sub-total in GBP			**500.00**	**1,000.00**	**250.00**			
5G / Digital proofs									
	SVABC12 / SUPPLIER 4								
	24/09/2003		003184	780.00	0.00	0.00			
	Sub-total in GBP			**780.00**	**0.00**	**0.00**			
	SVABC2 / SUPPLIER 3								
	12/08/2003	000144	DUMMY	0.00	312.00	0.00			IMAGE PROOFS
	Sub-total in GBP			**0.00**	**312.00**	**0.00**			
5J / Couriers & deliveries									
	SVAGCP / SUPPLIER 1								
	12/09/2003	003052	DUMMY	0.00	120.00	0.00			3 BIKES TO CITY- WAIT & RETURN
	Sub-total in GBP			**0.00**	**120.00**	**0.00**			
5K / Time of staff									
	1R4CSACJHAY / HAYES J.								
	05/10/2003	T040		0.00	2,530.00	0.00			HOURS=22.00
	Sub-total in GBP			**0.00**	**2,530.00**	**0.00**			
Total in GBP				**1,280.00**	**3,962.00**	**250.00**			

Source: Reproduced by permission of Donovan Data Systems 2005.

Figure 7.3   Dummy campaign work-in-progress report

Or certain small operators have more acute cashflow issues and have had experience of big companies exacerbating this. Consequently their policy is ask for money in advance.

- Mistakes can always be made on invoices: check invoices thoroughly and match up against estimates.
- Do not let invoices sit in your in-tray for weeks (that's one for all the external finance directors out there!).

Final Reconciliations

The campaign is out in the marketplace. You went on your holiday and caught up on all your sleep. Before you move onto the next campaign, make sure you get the agency to reconcile the job. This will highlight how the campaign eventually ran in terms of actual costs, if there is any money to be credited and what is yet to be invoiced (see Figure 7.4).

- Ask the agency to take you through this face-to-face.
- Every so often ask for third-party invoices to support the invoicing.
- Ask for the agency's time analysis to support the estimated project fee.
- Remember that the relationship is founded on trust, so do not use a reconciliation meeting as an inquisition rather than a forum for clarification.

COMMENT

You may at some point feel that you are not getting value for money from some aspects of the campaign development process. It is your money so you need to make sure you and the agency are being as efficient as possible. Therefore you may consider asking your procurement people, an external consultant or one of the third-party companies (as mentioned in Chapter 3) to run an *ad hoc* audit to measure the buying efficiency, use of suppliers, time taken, etc. Ultimately this can be time consuming, a little distracting for both sides and not in the spirit of a trusting partnership, so these should not be done on every campaign. And in fact to show partnership you may ask the agency in advance if it has any ways of making things more efficient in the campaign process, or to display its buying efficiency.

Reconciliation

We Do Great Work
A G E N C Y

Quarter 1 Campaign Cost Reconciliation
10/3/08

Campaign Element	Budget Cost	Actual Cost
Photography	€10 000	€9 900
Press Ad Production	€13 000	€16 000*
Media Space	€750 000	€750 000
Response Incentives	€31 000	€31 000
Inbound Response Handling	€40 000	€35 000
Agency Time (see attached breakdown)	€75 000	€75 000
Legal Approval	€500	€500
Purchase of new freephone number	€5 000	€5 000
Sundries	€5 000	€3 671.67
Contingency	€10 500	–
TOTAL	**€940 000**	**€926 071.67**

* Overrun due to change by sales department of pricing structure. Cost approved 3/02/08.

Figure 7.4 Sample campaign cost reconciliation

EXERCISES

1 Ask your agency to show you detailed time analysis for the last campaign reconciliation.

2 Review your internal purchase order and invoice sign-off procedures for efficiency.

3 Talk to the agency's finance director about any potential ways to gain any campaign efficiencies.

DEVELOPING A LONG-TERM RELATIONSHIP

CHAPTER 8

DEVELOPING A LONG-TERM RELATIONSHIP

In this chapter you will learn about:

- Managing creativity.
- Knowing the friction points.
- Balancing success and failure.
- Getting your portfolio of agencies to work together.
- Evaluating agency performance.

T he client–agency relationship is a dynamic organism which needs nurturing and sustaining in times of growth, change and adversity. You, as part of the partnership, are jointly responsible for giving the relationship direction and keeping things fresh. Whether you are a campaign manager or a marketing director, you can help the agency to give your company the best service and develop a rich seam of collaboration. Obviously, the agency and its management has a defined role to play in this as well but you, as the commissioner of its services, set the pace and tone for how it operates. Ultimately, there is a trust that needs to be built up between agency and client – and this works both ways.

Once a client is happy to let an agency take credit for business results, then you know that the relationship is working. But it takes a very long time for a client to be prepared to do that and for an agency to be able to demonstrate it. Yet, it is fundamental to agency–client relationships; it takes both parties beyond just doing campaigns and into the area of business partnership.

Consequently, you need to be aware of how the agency gels in the relationship, how to keep the relationship fresh and what you may encounter along the way. The task becomes more complicated when you have more than one agency or a wider geographical coverage. Whatever the setup, you will also need to evaluate the agency's performance to manage the relationship and allow the agency to give your company a 'value-added' service.

MANAGING CREATIVITY

It is a myth that creativity is the exclusive domain of the agency's creative department. Creativity is a method of solving problems in an imaginative, productive way and this challenge is probably the one single thing that defines why so many of us find marketing so fascinating. Creativity is therefore not a talent or skill you pick up at art school. If you understand (1) that creativity will be the driving force both in your dealings with the agency and in the campaign development process and (2) that this creativity has different components, then you can formulate how to harness it. Teresa Amabile has illustrated the key components in Figure 8.1.

Applying this model, you as the client have a part to play in the areas of *Expertise* and *Motivation*. The agency will have the skill and craft to develop and execute communications in general but you need to work out what you can provide that will help them to develop communications particularly for your company. Some of the ways to enhance the knowledge of the agency personnel have been mentioned in various other chapters but it is worth seeing them in their entirety here:

- Make sure that they have a clear understanding of the products they will be working on. (Can you get them to put the product on trial or spend time with a product specialist?)

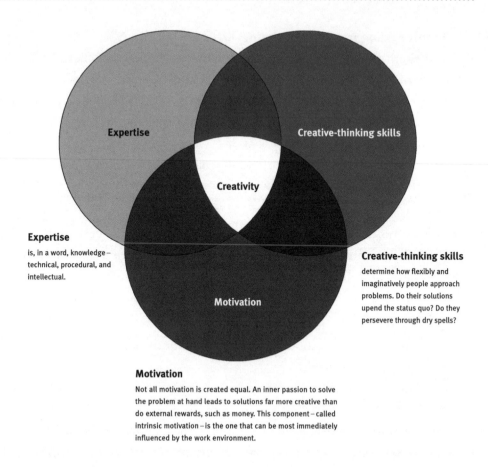

Expertise

Creative-thinking skills

Creativity

Expertise

Motivation

Creative-thinking skills

Expertise

is, in a word, knowledge – technical, procedural, and intellectual.

Creative-thinking skills

determine how flexibly and imaginatively people approach problems. Do their solutions upend the status quo? Do they persevere through dry spells?

Motivation

Not all motivation is created equal. An inner passion to solve the problem at hand leads to solutions far more creative than do external rewards, such as money. This component – called intrinsic motivation – is the one that can be most immediately influenced by the work environment.

Figure 8.1   The three components of creativity

- Immerse them in brand thinking. (Yes, they have the brand guidelines but have they spent time with the brand thought leader, e.g. the marketing director, CEO or other agency planner?)
- Review your major communications over the past five years. (They need to know where you have come from so that they can assess where you will be going.)
- Give them insight into your customers. (Invite them to focus groups and your call centre. Ask your customer data specialist to spend time with them.)
- Allow them to understand your distribution channels. (Suggest that they become 'mystery shoppers'.)

- Discuss pricing policy with them.
- Give them insight into competitive activity. (Encourage them to trial the competition as well. Invite them to trade shows or the equivalent.)
- Expose them to the individuals who are in your internal approval process. (Highlight some of the personal motivations and hot issues with these people.)
- Give them access to all the market information you hold (e.g. press clippings, market reports, showreels).

In terms of motivation, agency people are simple folk with very obvious 'hot-buttons'. They tend to be team players but they like individual attention and recognition. The following techniques are just as relevant for your colleagues but consider them in keeping the agency personnel motivated:

- Show them that their input is adding to the business. (Keep them regularly abreast of the sales results.)
- Show them your trust. (Maybe you do not need to be at all the meetings they hold with other departments.)
- Take them into your confidence. (This makes people feel valued and they will not need to be asked to exercise discretion.)
- Allow agency personnel to feel that they are challenging you positively. (Take that leap of faith occasionally.)
- Give praise in front of other agencies/departments, but not as an act of favouritism.
- Send an email to the appropriate account handler, creative, planner, etc., after the success of a campaign (copied, in particular, to his/her boss).
- Organize a thank-you drink to the team for their hard work. (Sure, they are paid to do this work but they will go even further next time if they see how much you value them.)
- Take a personal interest in the individuals in your agency. (I was grateful to a client for telling me about an under-publicized concert featuring one of my all-time favourite singers; it was worth 10 corporate lunches – he knew my tastes and gave me invaluable information.)

- Use any company perks for small rewards (e.g. car manufacturers will always be popular with the Formula 1 buffs).
- Surprise and delight your agency people every so often. (Maybe award them a project they would like to do but do not normally have in their remit.)
- Do not underestimate the social side of the relationship (asking what people are doing at the weekend, making time for a drink after the meeting).
- Shield the agency from any bullies in your company.
- Celebrate successes as a combined team.

COMMENT

Awards can play an important part in agency motivation and in showing the agency your commitment to innovative, results-driven creativity. There is a perception in the client world that the agency people are obsessed with awards. I wanted to comment on this – yes, we are but not as much as you think! I think there are a number of reasons for this. The agency community is very conscious of its peers and (going back to one of those 'hot-buttons') wants their recognition. This may lie in the fact that job-length in agencies is relatively short in comparison to that in client companies, so they crave more universal acknowledgement. Agency management is also very conscious that these provide not only motivation within the agency but also strong credentials for new business. With creative teams as well, their 'guardbook' of personal work and awards is the equivalent of most people's CVs. Therefore, an award is peer recognition and a mechanism for career progression.

On the less self-obsessed side, awards are primarily indicators of imagination, creativity and business success. They put your organization in the company of winners and promote your activity within the marketing industry. They can serve you just as well as they can agencies.

The worry from clients is that agencies think more about awards than about business results. The good news is that in reality agencies are not in the habit of putting awards ahead of what is best for their client business. And, as awards are geared to clients as much as to agencies, more and more awards schemes are ensuring that business results are integral in the main evaluation criteria. Therefore, my advice is to show the agency that, where relevant, you are committed to winning awards by creating results-driven work of a high standard, but using awards as recognition rather than as a sole objective.

KNOWING THE FRICTION POINTS

As in any relationship, there will always be areas of friction. If you know what these are, you will be more prepared for them. I am not saying that they will not occur but you will act differently with this knowledge.

Costs

This has to be the biggest area because it encapsulates so many elements and money is always going be a scarce resource. This has already been discussed in Chapter 7 and, as was highlighted, a good deal of this is about expectation management on both sides. With agency resource costs, you should establish the framework well in advance of any campaigns or you will be making expedient decisions in the heat of the fray. In terms of production, make sure that it is very clear what budget they have and that they need to let you know at all times of any extra cost implications. Be prepared for agencies not to move until a cost estimate is signed off or a purchase order is issued, as agencies have been severely burnt by the practice of running up costs without written approval.

There will always be unforeseen costs. You should be prepared in advance by making a contingency in the estimate. You should also question why these costs have occurred and know whether and why you should be paying for them. Sundry costs can mount up so you need to have confidence that your account handler is managing them. As a random check, you should say at the beginning of a particular campaign that at reconciliation stage you would like to see the individual costs to understand the total. If the agency knows about it in advance, then it can record them specifically (e.g. '€60 – overnight courier to HQ to deliver second–stage artwork to M. Jones' rather than just '€60 bike to Slough'). Asking for this on every occasion, however, will be a drain on time and resource and if there is trust, you should not need to do so. I always think it is one of the first death knells of a relationship when, long after the end of a big budget campaign, €200 worth of bikes are queried and the time to document them will actually exceed the delivery costs.

Time

This must be the other major friction point in negotiations, either at the start of the campaign or during it when you need to speed things up or something unforeseen threatens to push the schedule back. You and your agency should agree, at the outset of the relationship, what a typical campaign timing is and this should be adapted to the campaigns accordingly. If you need to 'shave' time off the overall period for a quick campaign, my thoughts go to an ex-colleague who always says that a problem well defined is a problem half solved. Therefore you should really keep the planning time the same and squeeze the other areas. Yet, what we tend to do, ironically, is reduce the front end because the back end production is less flexible.

If you agree to reduce the quality control time, make sure that those approving in your organization and the agency are lined up to provide a quick turnaround.

Creative Amends

These come in two stages at concept approval and in creative development (including artwork and digital production). The classic scenario is a conversation that starts 'We love the concept but we just want to change X'. X varies from (1) something inconsequential like the offer end date (which will have no bearing on the core idea), (2) incorporating an element from one of the other concepts they saw, to (3) 100% change, but just keeping the logo the same. The agency will have a problem with anything that detracts from the core idea. Therefore it may be worth defining the core idea and ensuring that it is still supported with the proposed change before you have your conversation with the agency. If the core idea is no longer there, it may be worth starting again or choosing another concept.

The other types of amendments are those at copy stage and in the visual image development. Of these, 80% are totally justified and should be effected effortlessly by the agency, but I would say there are 20% that do not add to the creative product and are not really necessary. Beware that you do not subject a good idea to the death of a thousand cuts. This can be either from your own subjectivity (see this in relation to evaluation in Chapter 5), from allowing other departments/colleagues to overstep their mark or poorly interpreted amendments. Something of which both the agency and client can be guilty is leaving the development of the project in very junior hands where amendments are just processed rather than thought about and dealt with smartly.

Try to avoid using artwork or digital production for major changes as this can be costly. Educate your colleagues that they need to give their input in the earlier development stages. If you know that this is inevitable, then alert the agency that this will be the case.

Production

Print, web and film production are complex procedures. We rely heavily on these to deliver the final project on budget and on time. In the heat of the campaign – particularly when the end date is in sight – you are at the mercy of the people who supervise the production. In industry folklore there are enough horror stories to send you screaming to an early grave. So I would say that it is very difficult to legislate for this friction point other than (1) to follow the general principles of project management, (2) to make sure you have confidence in your agency, colleagues and suppliers who manage the production process and (3) to learn enough about the techniques to enable you to hold an informed conversation when issues arise.

Attitude

Sometimes, for those who do not know them well, agency people can come over as a little too confident, talking in a language that often needs a codebreaker. You should be conscious of this in any encounters between them and your colleagues from other departments. Frequently, those in other departments can feel intimidated by the so-called 'black arts' of advertising and marketing, so ask the agency to be aware of this as well.

Agencies can come over as a little 'precious' when it comes to making certain changes and executing other requests. No doubt, you have one view and in the mind of the agency there is a good reason for any hesitation. The relationship should be founded on trust and mutual respect for each other's expertise – this is when an open, honest, emotion-free discussion is needed. Often when problems arise and stress or time close in, these discussions get missed, emotions build up and the friction festers. Make sure that you and the agency give yourselves the freedom to have such an open dialogue.

BALANCING SUCCESS AND FAILURE

As partners, you hope to achieve campaign success after campaign success. Yet in reality, in the type of work you produce, you will both need to take risks. On one hand this is incredibly exciting for you but there will be times when a campaign does not yield the success that was expected. Once again it is the way you handle and manage both success and lack of it, in your company or with the agency, that will colour the relationship. Celebration of success is an essential part of your existence together, but there is a way to do it that does not make other people think you have found the cure for cancer. Particularly within your company, there will be those whose expectations need to be managed. If a campaign success is vaunted too much, then future expectation could be too high. Similarly, if the campaign has not been successful, you need to manage the news internally. The best route is to have an initial understanding of why it did not work in order to be prepared for the questions. Then make sure you and the agency really explore the reasons to ensure that you do not repeat them in future.

This happened to our team recently. Initial leads for a particular client's niche campaign had been very low, so the contact centre was asked (1) to analyse the enquiries and (2) to see whether they had any sense of conversion to sales at such an early stage. What we were actually doing was getting ready for the client's senior management querying why such creative work (which both we and our client contact felt was excellent) had not produced the results. In this case, we were lucky and there was a happy ending. The leads had been low in volume but an outstanding sales conversion and non-trackable leads had contributed to a very successful campaign. However, it could have gone the other way and we would have to have been prepared accordingly.

With a campaign that is not as successful as expected, you have to make sure that you learn from the results and do not make the agency or other departments innocent scapegoats.

GETTING YOUR PORTFOLIO OF AGENCIES TO WORK TOGETHER

You may work with a number of agencies of different disciplines. You may have a roster of similar agencies who have to work together. Your company will nevertheless be paying out a good deal of money for these agencies and you will want to optimize the investment by making sure that they work well together and do not duplicate their coverage. For their part, agencies can be territorial, sometimes a little precious and always looking out for new income streams. Therefore how do you instil into them a sense of collaboration for a common good?

In my experience, the best situations have been where the client has been clear about the scope of individual activity and has created a joint operating framework. How you establish your framework depends on your individual situation. It starts with your choice of agencies. If you are looking for an agency which is apparently 'happy to collaborate' you need to see proof of this at credentials stage. The agency needs to show not only that it can work with other agencies but how in detail this actually happens and what benefits the clients have reaped. You may be shopping for agencies of different disciplines at the same time. If so, you could take the decision to go with sister agencies from the same group. Examples of common client work are also imperative; a number of agencies are 'sisters' in name only, but they can put up a good front. Nevertheless there are some partner agencies who work well and you have the advantage that they have already worked out their own *modus operandi* and lines of accountability.

TIP

As mentioned in Chapter 3, there is a current trend of workshop pitches where the potential client not only sees the agency in action but in the context of working with other agencies. If you have an established PR agency and trusted direct marketing agency and you are looking for a brand advertising agency, why not ask your existing agencies to partake in such a workshop? Admittedly these are hothouse conditions but you will still get a better sense of the potential collaborative spirit.

Once you have your agencies in place you will have to make a call as to how they input into the overall marketing strategy development. And this depends how you are set up and whether you wish to have the agency/agencies as part of the steering force. For example one option is that you have a strategic representative from each discipline match up with the equivalent from your company, and as a team you develop the combined strategy. Alternatively you have one agency as the 'thought leader' within the agencies and you include that agency in the marketing planning. The other agencies then take the lead from the 'thought leader' agency which, traditionally, has been the agency involved with the brand planning. Another option is that your company is strong enough to create the lead. You can then dispense the strategy to the agencies and certain internal functions (marketing strategy and brand guardian departments) should make sure that everyone is on track and consistent with the vision. What also determines your choice is the budget available to have an agency/agencies playing a quasi–internal role.

Whichever structure you choose, there is a risk that the agencies cannot work with each other, there is territorialism, there is lack of consistency in the communications, you are duplicating activity, etc. The way I have seen it work best is if clients establish a framework whereby they:

- Have annual and quarterly kick-off meetings to plan and launch activity.
- Make sure all agencies are up to speed with products, the brand and everybody's activity (this meeting can form part of team-building sessions).
- Ask, for example, the internal PR manager or the PR agency representative to encourage the integration of the PR function within the other agencies' thinking.
- Are aware of different campaign development lead-times to allow individual activity to dovetail.
- Do not encourage 'scope creep' from agencies. (It may save them some money in the short term but they may have more longer-term problems).
- Do not show favouritism to an agency in front of the other agencies (even if it is the thought-leader).
- Expose all agencies to the same market information, sales figures, or consumer research available.
- Understand the different agencies' strengths and weaknesses, playing to their strengths when allocating projects.
- Use the joint meetings to reinforce the vision, the collaborative spirit and the results they are jointly achieving.
- Keep financial arrangements out of the joint meetings.

COMMENT

One of the most difficult agency coordination tasks is where you have to work with an agency on a pan-continental or global basis. The basic principles still apply but, budgets aside, you need to have an agency network that mirrors both your decision-making structure and your implementation network. So if you are a brand operating out of London centrally with non-marketing satellites in the European capitals, you should employ an agency in London to develop communications centrally and have them translated/adapted for the local markets. However, if the local markets historically have had their own marketing autonomy, this format will not work. You will need to work with a network that will develop with you a *modus operandi* for campaign development which involves the local markets but ideally exploits cost-efficiencies.

In my experience of working on pan-European and global accounts, there are many complex answers to the various network scenarios. If this is new territory to you, you may wish to investigate and talk to other clients of your agency network to determine what could work best for your operation.

EVALUATING AGENCY PERFORMANCE

Some agency–client relationships just carry on with the momentum of the work or owing to certain individuals' personal chemistry. Ultimately these relationships will encounter problems if they do not formalize some sort of continuous evaluation. There have been some typical examples in the past where a senior marketer has appointed an agency and then moved on, and only after the client's departure did it come to light that there were a number of unresolved issues. In such a case, the successor may need to remedy things or, sadly, deal with the situation acutely by terminating the arrangement. Therefore generally it is better for both sides to establish formal and informal mechanisms to monitor the health of the relationship.

The benefits can be seen on both sides in the following:

* Identifying the role of the agency in working with its clients.
* Managing expectations in terms of service levels.
* Opening up two–way feedback channels.
* Identifying any problems in advance.

- Developing and strengthening relationships.
- Aiding accountability.
- Boosting individual morale and combined team motivation.

Monitoring agency performance should be seen in the overall framework of defining the parameters of the relationship, as presented in Figure 8.2.

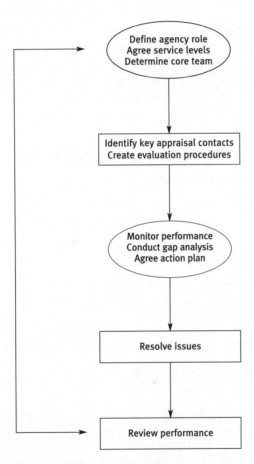

Figure 8.2   Stages of agency performance evaluation

Defining the Agency Role and its Service Levels

The role of the agency, core personnel and service level agreements are all interdependent decisions that are very much influenced by the budget allocated for agency involvement.

Determining the required agency input (see Figure 3.3 in Chapter 3) and the accompanying levels of service is a good initial 'stake in the ground' to allow agency performance to be evaluated. Areas where service levels may be agreed on both sides include:

- Establishment of core agency team.
- Timely turnaround of concepts from original client brief.
- Total campaign period.
- Timeliness of timing schedules and cost estimates after briefing.
- Frequency of status meetings and issue of contact/status reports.
- Submission of production quotes.
- Timing of purchase orders/invoicing procedures.
- Timing of client feedback.
- Working procedures with other agencies/departments.
- Adherence to brand guidelines.
- Use of certain suppliers.
- Adherence to certain project management standards/procedures (e.g. ISO 9000).
- Creative output.
- Contribution to marketing objectives.
- Contribution to business results.

Creating Evaluation Procedures

The most important point here is that the procedures do not become so rigid that you cannot phone your main agency contact to talk certain issues through. You and your agency need to make sure that there is continuous feedback on both sides and that it is in the spirit of *kaizen*, the philosophy of continuous improvement. Because some people feel more comfortable and qualified in communicating more formal feedback, you should identify who, in the agency, should be part of the performance monitoring process. On the agency side, the account director is normally the person responsible for ensuring the smooth running of day-to-day projects. Therefore she/he should be the first port of call for any feedback on day-to-day issues. For more long-term or serious conversations, there should be someone identifiable in the agency (e.g. client services director, agency management).

When you begin, formally, to review the agency's performance, you may wish to solicit the assistance of others. This can be done within your company (your boss, human resources or purchasing) or by the use of a number of consultants who have developed 360° evaluation techniques. Some of the third-party companies mentioned in Chapter 3 also specialize in this area.

In establishing a performance review, bear in mind the following:

- Consult all internal personnel/teams who work with the agency.
- Ask for written feedback and verbal clarification.
- Identify the evaluation criteria.
- Establish how feedback should be given:
    - Keep evaluation relevant.
    - Be specific and give examples.
    - Limit evaluation to what can be achieved in the future.
    - Include praise for individuals.
    - Comment on the action rather than the person.
    - Avoid overkill.
- Ask the agency for feedback on your team.
- Treat the review as a two-way opportunity.
- Use a written/electronic form as the basis for discussion.
- Make sure you have confirmed the time period being reviewed.
- Identify those factors that are outside the agency's control (e.g. internal budget cuts, change in marketing strategy).
- Confirm who will be at the meeting.
- Confirm process (feedback eliciting, evaluation meeting, development of corrective action plan and secondary meeting to review actions).
- Establish the frequency of evaluation meetings (e.g. 12-monthly period with 6-monthly informal meeting and 'action review' meetings).
- Conduct the review meeting so that people feel at ease and are free to air any issues.

An example of the sections of the agency evaluation form can be seen in Figures 8.3(a)–(f).

Agency Service Evaluation

Crazy For Work
L I M I T E D

Methodology

- Benchmark on agreed agency service criteria
- Agency service categories to include
  - Strategic planning
  - Creative output
  - Account management
  - Management involvement

- Allocate score to performance ratings

  5 = Excellent
  4 = Above expectations
  3 = Meets expectations
  2 = Below expectations
  1 = Unacceptable

- Agency service categories to be weighted accordingly

Creative	30%
Account management	30%
Strategic planning	30%
Management involvement	10%

Results

Covering time period _____

Personnel conducting evaluation _____

Personnel consulted _____

OVERALL AGENCY MEAN SCORE
(including weighting)

Overall priorities for the next 6 months

1. _____
2. _____
3. _____

Figure 8.3(a)   Example of the agency evaluation form: Agency service evaluation

Strategic Planning

Crazy For Work
L I M I T E D

	1 Excellent	2 Above expectations	3 Meets expectations	4 Below expectations	5 Unacceptable
1.1 Understanding of market and consumer trends	⬯	⬯	⬯	⬯	⬯
1.2 Understanding of client's business issues	⬯	⬯	⬯	⬯	⬯
1.3 Contribution to brand thinking	⬯	⬯	⬯	⬯	⬯
1.4 Ability to identify rich insights	⬯	⬯	⬯	⬯	⬯
1.5 Development of inspiring creative briefs	⬯	⬯	⬯	⬯	⬯
1.6 Adherence to budgets/timings	⬯	⬯	⬯	⬯	⬯
1.7 Establishing campaign benchmarks	⬯	⬯	⬯	⬯	⬯
1.8 Monitoring effectiveness of work	⬯	⬯	⬯	⬯	⬯
1.9 Cooperation/collaboration with other agencies /client departments	⬯	⬯	⬯	⬯	⬯

Overall mean score

_____

Comments   _____
             _____
             _____
             _____
             _____

Key priorities for the next 6 months

1.   _____

2.   _____

3.   _____

Figure 8.3(b)   Example of the agency evaluation form: Strategic planning

Creative Output

Crazy For Work
L I M I T E D

	1 Excellent	2 Above expectations	3 Meets expectations	4 Below expectations	5 Unacceptable
2.1 Appropriateness for brand	⬭	⬭	⬭	⬭	⬭
2.2 Adherence to propositions	⬭	⬭	⬭	⬭	⬭
2.3 Originality and impactfulness	⬭	⬭	⬭	⬭	⬭
2.4 Realizing concepts through to execution	⬭	⬭	⬭	⬭	⬭
2.5 Client access to creative personnel	⬭	⬭	⬭	⬭	⬭
2.6 Creative work delivering results	⬭	⬭	⬭	⬭	⬭

Overall mean score _____

Comments _____
_____
_____
_____
_____

Key priorities for the next 6 months

1. _____
2. _____
3. _____

Figure 8.3(c)   Example of the agency evaluation form: Creative output

Account Management

Crazy For Work
LIMITED

	1 Excellent	2 Above expectations	3 Meets expectations	4 Below expectations	5 Unacceptable
3.1 Understanding of market/business dynamics	◯	◯	◯	◯	◯
3.2 Smooth project management	◯	◯	◯	◯	◯
3.3 Adherence to timing	◯	◯	◯	◯	◯
3.4 Financial responsibility and efficiency	◯	◯	◯	◯	◯
3.5 Efficient administration	◯	◯	◯	◯	◯
3.6 Availability/accessibility	◯	◯	◯	◯	◯
3.7 Initiative taking	◯	◯	◯	◯	◯
3.8 Responsiveness to suggestions	◯	◯	◯	◯	◯
3.9 Commitment and enthusiasm	◯	◯	◯	◯	◯
3.10 Cooperation/collaboration with other agencies/client departments	◯	◯	◯	◯	◯

Overall mean score _____

Comments _____
_____
_____
_____
_____

Key priorities for the next 6 months

1. _____
2. _____
3. _____

Figure 8.3(d)   Example of the agency evaluation form: Account management

Management Involvement

Crazy For Work
L I M I T E D

	1 Excellent	2 Above expectations	3 Meets expectations	4 Below expectations	5 Unacceptable
4.1 Understanding of market/brand issues	⬭	⬭	⬭	⬭	⬭
4.2 Contribution to business/communication discussions	⬭	⬭	⬭	⬭	⬭
4.3 Involvement in relationship	⬭	⬭	⬭	⬭	⬭
4.4 Commitment/enthusiasm	⬭	⬭	⬭	⬭	⬭
4.5 Availability/accessibility	⬭	⬭	⬭	⬭	⬭
4.6 Promoting agency accountability	⬭	⬭	⬭	⬭	⬭

Overall mean score _____

Comments _____
_____
_____
_____
_____

Key priorities for the next 6 months

1. _____

2. _____

3. _____

Figure 8.3(e)   Example of the agency evaluation form: Management involvement

Agency Evaluation of Client

Crazy For Work
LIMITED

	1 Excellent	2 Above expectations	3 Meets expectations	4 Below expectations	5 Unacceptable
Clear and inspiring briefs					
Realistic timescales/budgets					
Willingness to adopt new ideas					
Clear and timely feedback					
Best use of agency resources					
Financial efficiency					
Effective meetings					
Access to relevant information					
Understanding of agency systems					
Sharing of market and business information					
Spirit of partnership					

Overall mean score _____

Comments _____
_____
_____
_____
_____

Figure 8.3(f)   Example of the agency evaluation form: Agency evaluation of client

EXERCISES

1   Assess your agency's policy on awards.

2   Identify whether your agency spends enough time with your brand's thought leader.

3   Review your agency's performance evaluation procedures.

EPILOGUE

What I have tried to give you in *Working with Agencies: An Insider's Guide* is a different perspective to creating a collaborative partnership with an agency. It was never intended as a revelation of trade secrets. On the contrary, I do not believe you can have those types of secrets in such a relationship. If you are to engender trust and mutual respect for each other's expertise, you need a platform of knowledge and transparency. You need to be able to pursue a sense of collaboration together, knowing that you can trust your partner.

It feels as if we are currently undergoing a change in the nature of the relationships between clients and agencies as clients become more experienced and more demanding and the agency world becomes more polarized with the consolidation of bigger communications groups and the coexistence of smaller independents. At the same time conversely, there seems more potential for the reality of the partnership detailed in the book. More clients are looking for like-minded business partners who can deliver accountability and shareholder value and, similarly, agencies wish to rise to the challenge and are throwing off their historic mantle of creative aloofness. In my research for the book, I have also seen that there is a huge resource, provided by the trade bodies and third-party companies, which can be tapped into by both sides to aid this partnership.

Working with Agencies is designed to be extremely practical for the very reason that although we can spend time theorizing about trust, knowledge and risk-taking, it is only in the day-to-day practice of briefing, creative evaluation, and team communication that we see such concepts in action. Ultimately, client and agency need to know how they can take responsibility for their side of the collaboration and it is in the detail that it comes out. If you look around in our industry, you can see that getting this partnership right can produce results. Therefore, I hope this book goes some way to explain how you and your agencies can initiate or continue similar success. Of course, if you have not done so already, you will need to take a leap of faith. If there is any secret to be disclosed, this is it.

Good luck!

REFERENCES

Amabile, Teresa M. (1998) 'How to Kill Creativity' *Harvard Business Review* (September–October), Boston, MA.

Butterfield, Leslie (ed.) (1999) *Excellence in Advertising*, Butterworth–Heinemann, Oxford.

DMA, IPA, ISBA, MCCA and the PRCA (2004) *Finding an Agency*, available via their websites.

IPA, ISBA, MCCA and PRCA (2004) *The Client Brief*, available via their websites.

Sheth, Jagdish and Sobel, Andrew (2000) *Clients for Life*, Simon & Schuster, New York.

Steel, Jon (1998) *Truth, Lies & Advertising*, John Wiley & Sons Inc., New York.

von Oech, Roger (1992) *Creative Whack Pack®*, U.S. Games Systems, Inc., Stamford, CT.

White, Roderick (June 2003) *Briefing Creative Agencies*, Admap, World Advertising Research Center Ltd, Henley on Thames.

USEFUL INFORMATION SOURCES

The following are trade bodies and organizations associated with raising standards in advertising and marketing. Have a look at their websites for training opportunities as well as for some very useful joint industry guidelines in such areas as research, briefing, pitching and developing legally compliant communications.

The Advertising Association	www.adassoc.org.uk
Advertising Standards Authority	www.asa.org.uk
Association of Publishing Agencies	www.apa.co.uk
British Design & Art Direction	www.dandad.org
British Exhibition Contractors Association	www.beca.org.uk
Broadcast Advertising Clearance Centre	www.bacc.org.uk
The Chartered Institute of Marketing	www.cim.co.uk
Commercial Radio Companies Association	www.crca.co.uk
Committee of Advertising Practice	www.cap.org.uk
The Communication, Advertising and Marketing Education Foundation	www.camfoundation.com
The Communications Agencies Federation	www.cafinfo.com
Direct Mail Information Service	www.dmis.co.uk
The Direct Marketing Association	www.dma.org.uk
Incorporated Society of British Advertisers	www.isba.org.uk
Institute of Sales and Marketing Management	www.ismm.co.uk
The Institute of Direct Marketing	www.theidm.com

Institute of Practitioners in Advertising	www.ipa.co.uk
Institute of Public Relations	www.ipr.org.uk
Institute of Sales Promotion	www.isp.org.uk
Internet Advertising Bureau UK	www.iabuk.net
The Market Research Society	www.mrs.org.uk
Marketing Communication Consultants Association	www.mcca.org.uk
The Marketing Society	www.marketingsociety.org.uk
Ofcom	www.ofcom.org.uk
The Public Relations Consultants Association	www.prca.org.uk
Radio Advertising Bureau	www.rab.co.uk
Radio Advertising Clearance Centre	www.racc.co.uk
Royal Mail	www.royalmail.com
Satellite & Cable Broadcasters Group	www.scbg.org.uk

ABOUT THE AUTHOR

Michael Sims is also the author of *Agency Account Handling: Avoiding Blood, Sweat and Tears*, a practical handbook for those in agency client servicing. He is currently a freelance consultant in the UK advising on agency/client relationships, agency pitches and strategic direction.

His agency career has included Partners Andrews Aldridge, Wunderman and Rapp Collins and he has worked with clients such as Avis, BT, Department of Health, Gillette, Jaguar, Lexus, Lloyds TSB, Telewest and Xerox. He was Client Services Partner at Partners Andrews Aldridge which was a relatively new agency when they were the first agency to secure Campaign Direct Agency of the Year, the DMA Grand Prix and Precision Marketing Agency of the Year at the same time. He was also associated with the ground-breaking work on Lexus and the Department of Health's anti-smoking campaign.

Mike has worked on traditional and digital campaigns, consumer and b2b brands and has run pan-European accounts. Prior to working in agencies, he was a teacher and then worked in training and development in the marketing industry.

More recently, his interest in training led him to develop the highly successful workshops which have helped a number of clients work with their agencies more effectively.

INDEX

118 118 directory enquiry service 37
360 degree relationship evaluations 142, 173
AA 87
AAR 6, 47, 51, 54
'above the line' agencies 137
access issues, agencies 6–7, 8, 175–9
account handlers *see* client services
account management, agency evaluation forms 174–9
account planners 30, 34–5, 88–90, 138
  functions 30, 34–5
  skills 34–5
accountability issues 5–7, 168–9, 171–9
accountants 39
ad designs 98, 108
'adcepts' 42
added value 4–5, 9, 13–15, 28, 31–2, 98–9, 141, 181
administration
  agency efficiencies 146–7, 151–3, 175–9
  project management 118, 121–4, 146–7, 151–3, 175–9
advertising
  agencies 3–4, 168–9
  budgets 144–5
  measuring 98

Advertising Standards Authority (ASA) 98, 125–6
agencies
  see also relationships; selection...
  access issues 6–7, 8, 175–9
  accurate campaign estimates 149–51, 153–4, 164, 170–9
  administrative efficiencies 146–7, 151–3, 175–9
  assessment issues 7–8, 51–3, 56–68
  attributes 15–16
  awards 6, 63–8, 106, 108–9, 163
  background 3–23, 27–44, 47–71, 135–55, 159–80, 181–2
  behind the scenes 27–44
  briefings 6–7, 9, 13, 34–5, 40, 42, 75–92, 97, 108, 120–1, 124–5, 127–32, 179, 181
  brochures 64
  campaign budgeting 147–9
  challenging behaviour 14–16, 87–90, 162–3
  charm 69
  client requirements 5–8, 13–16, 27–8, 47–71, 146–7, 159–80
  commissions 136–7
  confidentiality issues 50, 56
  contacts 21–3, 123–4

agencies (*continued*)
contracts 28–9, 50, 62–8, 135–6, 143–4
creative aloofness 6–7, 13, 166, 181
creative briefings 40, 42, 76–92, 108, 120–1, 127–32
decision matrix 51–3
deliverables 5–7
emotion/induction curves 16–19
estimated costs 149–51, 153–4, 164
evaluations 7–8, 9, 51–3, 56–68, 70–1, 142, 160, 170–9, 181
'experts for hire' 13–16
feedback 65–8, 70–1, 103–8, 130–2, 162–3, 170–9
final reconciliations 153–4
finance 135–55, 164–6
functions 28–44
global networks 170
handovers 49, 80
hourly rates 138–9, 145–6, 149–50
industry guidelines 48–71
integration needs 6–8, 18, 28, 55, 68, 69–70, 160, 167–70, 175–9
invoices 146–7, 149, 151–3
legal issues 28–9, 98–9, 125–7, 143–4, 149–50, 154
longlists 51–2, 64
motivation buttons 160–3, 171–9
negative perceptions 145–6
new relationships 16–19, 54–71
origins 28–9
payment by results 139–40
performance issues 7–8, 21, 40–4, 139–40, 160, 170–9
phased fees 137–9
portfolios 167–70
presentations 18, 47–71, 99–106, 109–13, 127–30
project fees 139
project managers 128, 171–9
remuneration structures 135–40, 144
reputations 6, 8, 12, 53, 56, 145–6

requirements 6–8, 13–16, 27–30, 37, 47–71, 146–7, 159–80
returns 5, 7, 13
reviews 47–71, 118, 167, 170–9
role-definition evaluation 171–9
scoring matrices 7–8
service level agreements 170–9
shortlists 48–9, 56–8, 61–8
structure factors 28–44
surprise principles 83–4, 163
third-party specialists 49–52, 54–9, 139, 153
'thought leader' agencies 169–70
'trusted advisers' 13–16
types 3–4, 12–13, 33, 35, 55, 59–60, 125–6, 136–7, 144, 168–9
visits 17–18, 64
WIP reports 151–3
Agency Assessments International 54
Agency Insight 54
Amabile, Teresa M. 160–1
amendments, creative amends 130–1, 165–6
AMV.BBDO 4
approval processes 40–4, 78, 97, 108–9, 119, 120–1, 124–5, 129–30
Archimedean principle 76–7
ARS Persuasion® 98
art buyers, creative services 38
art directors, creative teams 35–6, 42–3
art exhibitions 108
Art Fund campaigns 91, 99–100, 104–5
artwork 30–1, 38–9, 124–5, 165–6
artwork-studio functions 30, 38–9
ASA *see* Advertising Standards Authority
assisted pitches, selection issues 56–8
attitudes, friction points 166
attributes, background 81–2, 98–9, 103–4
'audience' perspectives 86, 103–4, 147
audience-connection guidelines, presentations 109–13
audits, costs 146–7, 153–4

awards
  agencies 6, 63–8, 106, 108–9, 163
  objectives 163
'awaydays' 62

BA 88
barriers, relationships 6–8, 38–9,
    129–32, 138–9, 164–79
Bass 81–2
BBH 13
behind the scenes, agencies 27–44
'below the line' agencies 137
benchmarking 8, 12, 21, 41–2, 76–7,
    108–9, 139, 174
best practice 79–84, 142–3
Big Brother (TV series) 57
big ideas 99–101, 106–7, 109–13, 165
the big picture 146
black and white visuals 42–3
BMP 34
    see also DDB...
'brain dump' 75–6
brainstorming sessions 41–2, 62–3
brand teams *see* client services
brands 8, 12, 19, 41–4, 51–2, 79–84,
    98–102, 161–3, 178–9
    see also products
    agency reviews 51–2
    definitions 81–2
    good-briefing principles 79–84
    terminology 81–2
    understanding 81–2, 161–3, 178–9
briefings 6–7, 9, 13, 34–5, 40–4,
    75–92, 96–106, 172, 177–9, 181
    see also campaign...; creative...
    aims 76–9
    background 40–4, 75–92, 96–106,
        172, 177–9
    best practice 79–84
    brands 79–84
    clarity needs 80–4, 177–9
    collaborative framework 79
    'creative starters for ten' 92
    definition 76

focus principles 83–4
good principles 79–84
hotspots 84–7
increasing-distortion problems 78
inspiration 87–92, 98, 179
key elements 76–7, 79–80
propositions 81–2, 87–90, 97,
    110–11, 125
relay races 78–9
shared thinking 88–90
stages 76–9
success factors 91–2
surprise principles 83–4, 163
types 40–4, 76–9
where-are-we-now/where-do
    -we-want-to-be section
    headings 79–80
written briefs 50, 56, 59–68, 80
brochures, agencies 64
budgets 5, 9, 31–2, 98–9, 120–7,
    136–8, 144–51, 169, 177–9
    see also costs
    background 144–51, 169, 177–9
    multiple agencies 169
    setting procedures 144–5
business models 4
business-to-business (B2B) 8–9, 12
business-understanding needs, client
    requirements 5–8, 15, 17–18,
    27–8, 55, 59–68, 69–70, 160–3,
    175–9

call centres 15, 17–18, 147–50, 154
Campaign 106, 108
campaign briefings
    see also briefings
    background 40, 42, 75–92, 96–106,
        109, 117–32, 172, 177–9
    definition 76
    disguised examples 88–90
campaign budgeting, agency
    finances 147–9
campaign execution
    background 127–32, 176–9

campaign execution (*continued*)
  effective progression 127–32
  ideas 106
campaigns 5–8, 9–11, 18, 31, 40–4, 53,
  75–92, 96–106, 109, 117–32,
  135–55, 164–6, 179, 181–2
  see also project management
  approval processes 40–4, 78, 97,
    108–9, 119, 120–1, 124–5,
    129–30
  background 40–4, 53, 75–92,
    117–32
  creative development processes 40–4,
    75–92, 120–1, 127–32, 145–54,
    164–6, 179
  effective preparations 117–32
  failures 167
  finance 18–19, 30, 39, 61, 95–6,
    135–55
  legal issues 18, 28–9, 95–6, 98–9,
    118–19, 121–2, 124–7, 143–4,
    149–50, 154
  milestones 40–4, 120, 124–5, 164
  reviews 118, 121–2, 170–9
  smoothing the way 117–32
  success factors 21, 91–2, 162–3, 167,
    181–2
Cannes Lions 108
CAP *see* Committee of Advertising
cashflows 151–3
celebrations, relationships 18–19,
  162–3, 167
CEOs *see* chief executive officers
challenging behaviour 14–16, 87–90,
  162–3
championing processes, creative
  products 95–113
changes
  continuous improvements 172–3
  continuous learning 15–16
  information sources 63–8
  landscape 63–8
  relationships 4–5, 49–71, 181
charm, agencies 69

Chartered Institute of Marketing
  (CIM) 77
chemistry issues
  client requirements 5–8, 28–30,
    48–9, 55, 56–8, 68–71, 159–80
  face-to-face chemistry 56–8, 68–70,
    123–4, 130–1, 149, 153
chief executive officers (CEOs) 62–3,
  161
CIM *see* Chartered Institute of
  Marketing
clarity needs
  briefings 80–4, 177–9
  feedback 107, 173, 177–9
  presentations 109–13
  project management 118–24
  selection issues 61–8
client services 29–33, 76–7, 146–8,
  162–3, 172–9
  finance 146–8
  functions 29–32, 76–7
  levels 31
  skills 32–3
  typical day 31
clients
  see also organizations; relationships
  access issues 6–7, 8, 175–9
  agency requirements 6–8, 13, 27–8,
    159–80
  background 3–23, 159–80, 181–2
  campaign briefings 40, 42, 75–92,
    96–106, 109, 117–32, 172,
    177–9
  finance 18–19, 30, 39, 61, 95–6,
    135–55
  global networks 170
  legal issues 18, 28–9, 95–6, 98–9,
    118–19, 121–2, 124–7, 143–4,
    154
  procurement issues 49–50, 53,
    140–3, 153
  requirements 5–8, 13–16, 27–8,
    47–71, 146–7, 159–80
  visits 17–19, 64

Clients for Life (Sheth & Sobel) 13–14

COI 97

collaborative partnerships

  see also partnerships; relationships

  added value 4–5, 9, 13–15, 28,
    31–2, 98–9, 141, 181

  background 4–5, 8, 9, 13–16, 48, 79,
    117–18, 159–80, 181

  benefits 4–5, 9, 13–15, 48, 181

  essential spirit 13–16, 168

  'experts for hire'/'trusted
    advisers' 13–16

  responsibilities 4–5, 132, 146–7,
    159–60, 168, 181–2

commissions 136–7

commitment factors

  agency selection 61–8

  new teams 20, 29–30, 62–8

  project management 122–4, 175–9

Committee of Advertising (CAP) 125–6

common goals, new teams 20, 62–8

Communication Directors' Forum 63

communications 3–7, 9–23, 27–8,
    32–7, 50, 56, 66–71, 77–92, 96,
    101–2, 118–27, 130–2, 144–9,
    162–3, 181–2

  account planners 34–5

  agency reviews 50, 56, 66–8, 167

  breakdowns 6–7, 130–2, 138–9,
    164–6

  briefings 40, 42, 77–92

  customers 3–4, 9–12, 34–5, 85–6,
    96

  feedback 65–8, 70–1, 103–8,
    130–2, 162–3, 170–9

  internal communications 9–12,
    82–3, 122–4, 140–3

  interpersonal skills 12, 32, 122–3,
    131–2, 162–3

  legal issues 125–7

  objectives 119, 144–5, 147–9

  project management 118–26, 130–2

  propositions 81–2, 87–90

  protocol factors 20

reviews 50, 56, 66–8, 161–2, 167

SMART objectives 85

status meetings 122, 172

teams 9–12, 18–23, 29, 32, 34–5,
    66–8, 69–71, 77–92, 119–20,
    123–4, 181–2

unsolicited messages 51, 77

company perks 163

competence factors, new teams 20–1

competitor companies, landscape
    changes 63–8, 162

complaints log 121–2

concept-development stage, creative
    teams 36, 42, 97

concept-execution stage, creative
    teams 36, 42–3, 127–32

concepts 36, 42–3, 96–106, 111–13,
    127–32

confidentiality issues, agency reviews 50,
    56

Consultancy Management Standard 59

contacts, agencies 21–3, 123–4

context-understanding needs 27–8

contingency plans 120–1, 146–7,
    149–50, 154, 164–5

continuous evaluations 170–9

continuous improvements 172–3

continuous learning, trusted
    advisers 15–16

contracts

  agencies 28–9, 50, 62–8, 135–6,
    143–4

  models 144

conviction attributes, trusted
    advisers 15–16

copywriters

  creative teams 35–6, 42–3

  lawyers 126

core teams 18–23, 171–9

correspondence, project
    administration 121–2, 146

costs 5, 9, 31–2, 98–9, 120–7, 136–8,
    144–51, 153–4, 164–6

  see also budgets; finance

costs (*continued*)
  audits 146–7, 153–4
  estimates 149–51, 153–4, 164
  final reconciliations 153–4
  friction points 164–6
  overruns 146–7, 153–4, 164–5
  record-keeping needs 146–7, 149–50
  standard templates 149–51
creative aloofness, agencies 6–7, 13,
    166, 181
creative amends 130–1, 165–6
Creative Brief 54
creative briefings 40, 42, 76–92, 97,
    108, 120–1, 124–5, 127–32, 179
  see also briefings
  approval 78, 97, 124–5, 129–30
  creative development processes 40,
    42, 76–92, 108, 120–1, 127–32,
    179
creative development processes 40–4,
    75–92, 120–1, 127–32, 145–54,
    164–6, 179
creative directors 19, 36, 106, 124–5,
    130–1, 172–3
creative evaluations 7–8, 9, 96–106,
    176–9, 181
'Creative Inspiration' talks 109
creative materials research 107–8
creative presentations, guidelines 102–6,
    109–13
creative products 7–8, 9, 95–113,
    127–8, 164–6, 176–9, 181
  agency reviews 53, 66, 167, 170–9
  amendments 130–1, 165–6
  audience perspectives 103–6, 110
  championing processes 95–113
  checklist 98–9, 127–8, 176–9
  engagement issues 105–6
  evaluations 7–8, 9, 96–106, 176–9,
    181
  opinions 105–6
  presentations 102–6, 109–13,
    127–30
  receptive environments 108–9

research benefits 107–8
respect factors 105–6
creative rationale 111–13
Creative Review 108
creative services, functions 30, 38
'creative starters for ten', briefings 92
creative teams 30, 35–6, 42–3, 76–92,
    130–1
  briefings 42–3, 76–92
  functions 30, 35–6, 42–3, 76–7,
    130–1
  intimidation problems 36, 166
  relationships 36, 42–3, 130–1, 165–6
creative training courses 109
Creative Whack Pack® (Roger von
    Oech) 109
creative-thinking skills 160–3
creativity 5–12, 160–3, 181
  background 160–3
  client requirements 5–8, 55, 69–70,
    160–3, 174–9
  internal interviews 11–12
  key components 160–1
  management issues 160–3
cultural issues 5–8, 9–12, 32–3, 69–70,
    120, 170
  client requirements 5–8, 55, 69–70,
    160–3
  global relationships 170
  internal interviews 9–12
  teams 119–20
customers
  'audience' perspectives 86, 103–4
  briefings 83–6
  communications 3–4, 9–12, 34–5,
    85–6, 96
  insight 83–7, 101–2, 110–11, 161–2
  needs 11–12, 83–6
  surprise principles 83–4, 163

data planners, functions 37
Data Protection Act 126
databases 37
DDB London 13, 34

deadlines 38–9, 43–4, 85, 120–32, 147, 164–5, 172, 175–9
debriefs, agency reviews 51
decision matrix, agency reviews 51–3
decision-making guidelines, selection issues 62–8
deconstruction processes, presentations 111
deep-generalist attributes, trusted advisers 15–16
deliverables, agencies 5–7
designers 35–6
Diaz, Cameron 53
differentiating attributes, brands 81–4, 98–9, 103–4
digital agencies 33, 35
digital-production functions 38–9, 44, 165–6
diplomacy skills 131
direct mail 77, 112–13
direct marketing agencies 35, 55, 125–6, 144, 168–9
distribution departments 95, 161–2
distribution stage, campaign development processes 40, 44, 120–1, 127–32, 161–2
diversity issues, relationships 4–5, 33
DMA 48, 50, 59–68, 126, 140
documentation benefits, project management 121
dominant partners 4–5
'down-to-earthness' qualities 70
Duckworth, Gary 76–7
dynamics
    operations 5
    relationships 159–60
    teams 69–71, 96, 119–24, 159–60

Earnings Before Interest and Tax (EBIT) 139
econometric modelling 145
The Economist 4, 131
EHS Brann 4
emails 77, 123, 131, 162

emotions 15–19, 21–3, 124, 166
    emotion/induction curves 16–19
    empathy requirements 15–16, 21–3
employees, creative products 104, 162–3
engagement issues, creative products 105–6
enthusiasm, evaluations 106, 178–9
environmental-controls principles, presentations 109–13
equipment needs, presentations 110–11
estimates, costs 149–51, 153–4, 164
evaluations
    see also reviews
    360 degree relationship evaluations 142, 173
    agencies 7–8, 9, 51–3, 56–68, 70–1, 142, 160, 170–9, 181
    background 7–8, 9, 64–8, 70–1, 96–106, 142, 160, 170–9, 181
    continuous evaluations 170–9
    creative products 7–8, 9, 96–106, 176–9, 181
    criteria determination 97–102, 170–9
    forms 64–8, 70–1, 97–102, 172–9
    objective systems 61–2
    organizations 9–12, 142
    preparations 96–106
    procedures 7–8, 64–8, 70–1, 97–102, 172–9
    scoring matrices 7–8
    standardized evaluations 64–8, 70–1, 97–9, 172–9
events' coordinators 43, 55
Excel spreadsheets 149
Excellence in Advertising (Duckworth) 76–7
execution see campaign execution
expectation management 146–7, 164–6, 170–9
expertise component, creativity 160–3
'experts for hire', 'trusted advisers' evolution 13–15

Express Train 6
Extreme 108

face-to-face meetings 56–8, 68–70,
    123–4, 130–1, 149, 153
facilitators 120
failures 62–3, 68, 70–1, 167
fairness 27–8
feasibility, creative products 99, 127
feedback 65–8, 70–1, 103–8, 130–2,
    162–3, 170–9
  clarity needs 107, 173, 177–9
  creative products 103–8, 130, 162–3
  guidelines 106–8, 131–2, 162–3, 173
  post-pitch feedback forms 65–8,
      70–1
  problem explanations 107, 130
  selection issues 65–8, 70–1
film production 166
final products, viewings 128
final reconciliations, agencies 153–4
finance 5, 9, 18–19, 30, 31–2, 39, 61,
    95–6, 98–9, 120–7, 135–55, 164–6
  see also costs
  agencies 135–55, 164–6
  background 18–19, 30, 39, 61, 95–6,
      135–55, 164–6
  budgets 5, 9, 31–2, 98–9, 120–7,
      136–8, 144–51, 169, 177–9
  contracts 28–9, 50, 62–8, 135–6,
      143–4
  departments 18–19, 30, 39, 61, 95–6
  estimated costs 149–51, 153–4, 164
  final reconciliations 153–4
  invoices 146–7, 149, 151–3
  procurement issues 49–50, 53,
      140–3, 153
  relationships 135–55, 164–6
  remuneration structures 135–40, 144
  stages 145–54
finish requirements, visuals 97
fit considerations, client
    requirements 5–8, 55, 69–70

flexibility needs, project
    management 123–4, 128
fluctuations, relationships 3–4
FMCG 8–9, 97–8
focus
  good-briefing principles 83–4
  groups 107–8
football analogies 29
Ford 4
forecast sales, budget-setting
    procedures 144–5
fragmented structures 4
FT Creative Business 108

GAP analysis 12
global marketing directors 5–8
global networks, relationships 170
gut instincts 96, 99, 103–4, 106

handovers, agencies 49, 80
The Haystack Group 54
'helicopter vision' 146
HHCL 87
honesty 13, 15–16, 21, 107, 125–6,
    142, 166
Hoover flights promotion 125
hotspots, briefings 84–7
hourly rates, agencies 138–9, 145–6,
    149–50
HSBC 88

IBM 5
ideas 87–92, 98–100, 106–7, 109–13,
    165
identity, brand definitions 81–2
Imagination 4
implementation guidelines, agency
    selection 62–8
in-house artwork studios 39
increasing-distortion problems,
    briefings 78
induction/emotion curves 16–19
industry guidelines, agency
    reviews 48–71

information
    see also knowledge
    useful information sources 48, 59,
        63–8, 106, 108–9, 126, 143, 144,
        185–6
initial meetings, selection issues 56
insight, customers 83–7, 101–2,
    110–11, 161–2
'Insoles' direct mail 112–13
inspiration, background 87–92, 98,
    103–4, 109, 179
integration needs, client
    requirements 6–8, 18, 28, 55, 68,
    69–70, 160, 167–70, 175–9
integrity attributes, trusted
    advisers 15–16
interim benchmarks, new teams 21
internal interviews, questions 9–12,
    82–3
Internet 54, 77, 123, 131, 143, 144–5,
    185–6
    see also emails; web...
interpersonal skills 12, 32, 122–3,
    131–2, 162–3
interviews 9–12
intimidation problems, creative
    teams 36, 166
investments, returns 5, 7, 13
invoices 146–7, 149, 151–3
IPA 48, 50, 59–68, 79, 106, 140, 144
    Advertising Effectiveness Awards 106
    PBR guidelines 140
ISBA 48, 50, 59–68, 79, 109, 138–9,
    140, 142–4
ISO 9000 172

joint industry guidelines, agency
    reviews 48–71
judgement attributes, trusted advisers 16

kaizen 172–3
'kick-off' meetings 119, 169
The Kiss (Rodin) 99

knowledge 5–8, 12, 15–16, 21–3, 37,
    53, 108–9, 160–3, 181
    see also information
    agency contacts 21–3, 123–4
    client requirements 5–8, 27–8, 37,
        53, 55, 59–68, 69–70, 146–7,
        160–3, 175–9
    enhancement methods 160–1

last-minute requests, selection issues 64
lateral thinking 35
Lawmark 126
legal issues 18, 28–9, 95–6, 98–9,
    118–19, 121–2, 124–7, 143–4,
    149–50, 154
    communications 125–7
    contracts 28–9, 50, 62–8, 135–6,
        143–4
lessons learned 167
leverage concepts 76–7
Levi's 13
Lexus GB 43, 86
listening skills, internal interviews 12
Lloyds TSB 112–13, 141
location guidelines, presentations 110
longlists, agencies 51–2, 64
losers, selection issues 62–3, 68, 70–1
'Lunch and Learn' talks 109

Mac visuals 35–6, 42–3
Marketing 106
marketing departments 9–12, 95–6,
    140–3
    GAP analysis 12
    internal interviews 9–12
    skills 9–12, 131
marketing directors 5–8
Marketing Forum 63
marketing press 3–4, 63–8
marketing vision 6–8, 33, 85, 146
marketplace knowledge, client
    requirements 5–8, 27–8, 37, 53,
    55, 59–68, 69–70, 146–7, 160–3,
    175–9

MCCA 48, 50, 59−68, 79, 126, 140
media
  see also press; TV...
  planners 37
  selections 147
meetings
  face-to-face meetings 56−8, 68−70,
    123−4, 130−1, 149, 153
  guidelines 123−4, 172−3
  'kick-off' meetings 119, 169
  project management 119, 121−4
  reviews 56, 172−3
  status meetings 122, 172
  'wash-up' meetings 121−2
Mercedes 91
mergers and acquisitions 68
messages, bombardment statistics 77
milestones
  agency reviews 48−9
  campaigns 40−4, 120, 124−5, 164
milk products 84
mindsets, presentations 102−6
mission 20
Mother 32−3
motivation buttons 160−3, 171−9
multi-viewpoint perspectives,
    presentations 110
multiple treatments,
    presentations 127−8
mutual respect 7, 13, 15−16, 27−8,
    122−3, 166, 181
Myers−Briggs Type Indicator®
    assessments 21
'mystery shoppers' 161−2

Naked 37
National Gallery 99−100, 105
National Portrait Gallery 91
negative perceptions 145−6
new agencies 16−19, 54−71
new teams 18−23, 40−4, 62−71
  see also teams
  key factors 18−23, 62−8
'nightmare pitches' 63

objectives 40−2, 79−80, 85, 101−2,
    118−24, 144−5, 147−9
  awards 163
  communications 119, 144−5, 147−9
  project management 118−24
  SMART objectives 85
  strategic planning 40−2, 168−9, 179
  tasks 144−5
  where-are-we-now/where-do
    -we-want-to-be briefing
    headings 79−80
Ogilvy, David 87−8, 99
'one-stop shops' 28, 50
operations, dynamics 5
opinions, creative products 105−6
organizations
  see also clients
  background 8−12, 82−3, 95−113,
    140−3, 163
  evaluations 9−12, 142
  finance 18−19, 30, 39, 61, 95−6,
    135−55
  GAP analysis 12
  internal interviews 9−12, 82−3
  nature 8−12
  skills 9−12
origins, agencies 28−9
outside help *see* third-party specialists
oversell dangers, presentations 111
ownership responsibilities 119

P&G 97
pan-continental networks 170
Partners Andrews Aldridge 43, 112−13
partnerships 3−8, 13−16, 48, 117−32,
    159−80, 181−2
  see also collaborative partnerships
  dominant partners 4−5
payment by results (PBR),
    agencies 139−40
performance issues
  agencies 7−8, 21, 40−4, 139−40,
    160, 170−9

benchmarking 8, 12, 21, 41–2, 76–7, 108–9, 139, 174
  remuneration structures 139–40
  service level agreements 170–9
personality, background 81–2, 101
perspectives 86, 103–4, 110
phased fees 137–9
photography 127–8, 148, 150–1, 154
pitch issues
  agency reviews 47–71
  evaluation forms 65–8, 70–1
Pitt, Brad 53
planners see account planners
Pollitt, Stanley 34
portfolios, agencies 167–70
positioning, brands 81–2, 127
post-pitch feedback forms 65–8, 70–1
posters 42
PowerPoint® presentations 47–8, 109, 125
PR agencies 3–4, 12–13, 33, 55, 95, 144, 168–9
PRCA 48, 50, 59–68, 140
pre-order samples/tapes/run-outs 128
pre-production meetings 43
presentations
  agencies 18, 47–71, 99–106, 109–13, 127–30
  agency-selection factors 68–70
  audience-connection principles 109–13
  clarity needs 109–13
  creative products 102–6, 109–13, 127–30
  creative rationale 111–13
  debriefs 51
  deconstruction processes 111
  effectiveness guidelines 109–13
  environmental-controls principles 109–13
  equipment needs 110–11
  good principles 109–13
  location guidelines 110
  mindsets 102–6
  multi-viewpoint perspectives 110
  multiple treatments 127–8
  oversell dangers 111
  packs 111
  preparations 109–13
  proposals 18, 66
  questions 111–13
  rehearsals 109–10
  stages 110–13
press
  ads 15, 42, 131–2, 148–50, 154
  marketing press 3–4, 63–8
  releases 50, 56, 143
  runs 128
print departments 18, 118, 149, 166
problem-solving roles 129, 160
procedures, project management 118, 120–4
procurement issues, background 49–50, 53, 140–3, 153
production function, creative services 38, 165–6
production stage
  campaign development processes 40, 44, 120–1, 127–32, 164–6
  friction points 164–6
products 17–18, 53, 77–9
  see also brands
  creative products 7–8, 9, 95–113, 127–8, 181
  final products 128
  induction benefits 17–18
  marketing briefs 77–9
programmers 35–6, 39
project fees 139
project management 9, 12, 30–5, 44, 69–70, 79–80, 117–32, 171–9
  administration 118, 121–4, 146–7, 151–3, 175–9
  agencies 128, 171–9
  approval processes 119, 120–1, 124–5, 129–30

project management (*continued*)
  background 117–32, 171–9
  clarity needs 118–24
  communications 118–25, 130–2
  complaints log 121–2
  deadlines 38–9, 43–4, 85, 120–32, 147, 164–5, 175–9
  documentation benefits 121
  establishment 118–24
  flexibility needs 123–4, 128
  goals 118–24
  meetings 119, 121–4
  milestones 120–1, 124–5, 164
  problems 123–4, 128–32, 170–9
  procedures 118, 120–4
  roles 118–24
  status meetings 122, 172
  teams 118–32
  'wash-up' meetings 121–2
proposals, presentations 18, 66
propositions
  background 81–2, 87–90, 97, 101–2, 103–7, 110–11, 125, 176–9
  brand definitions 81–2
  briefings 81–2, 87–90, 97, 110–11, 125
  checklist 87, 176–9
  strapline contrasts 81
protocol factors, new teams 20
psychometric assessments, teams 20–1, 119
publicity considerations, agency reviews 50, 56
purchase orders 149, 151–3
purchasing departments 49–50, 53, 140–3

quality controls 40–4, 120–1, 124–5, 127–32, 165
questions
  internal interviews 9–12, 82–3
  longlist questionnaires 51–2
  presentations 111–13

receptive environments, creative products 108–9
record-keeping needs, costs 146–7, 149–50
references 183
rehearsals, presentations 109–10
relationships 3–23, 27–32, 38–9, 48–71, 122–3, 129–32, 135–55, 159–80, 181
  see also collaborative partnerships
  agency-selection management 62–8
  background 3–23, 27–32, 38–9, 62–71, 122–3, 138–9, 159–80, 181
  barriers 6–8, 38–9, 129–32, 138–9, 164–79
  celebrations 18–19, 162–3, 167
  changes 4–5, 49–71, 181
  client services 29–32
  context-understanding needs 27–8
  contracts 28–9, 50, 62–8, 135–6, 143–4
  creative teams 36, 42–3, 130–1, 165–6
  diversity issues 4–5, 33
  dominant partners 4–5
  dynamics 159–60
  'experts for hire'/'trusted advisers' 13–16
  face-to-face chemistry 56–8, 68–70, 123–4, 130–1, 149, 153
  finance 135–55, 164–6
  fixability matrix 51–3
  fluctuations 3–4
  friction points 38–9, 129–32, 138–9, 164–79
  global networks 170
  good platforms 16–19, 159–80
  integration needs 6–8, 18, 28, 55, 68, 69–70, 160, 167–70, 175–9
  legal issues 28–9, 143–4, 149–50, 154
  new relationships 16–19

problems 6–8, 38–9, 129–32,
    138–9, 164–79
reviews 48–71
social side 163
'thought leader' agencies 169–70
trust 5, 6–7, 12, 13–15, 23, 122–3,
    146, 159–60, 162, 166–9, 181
relay races, briefings 78–9
remuneration structures,
    agencies 135–40, 144
reputations, agencies 6, 8, 12, 53, 56,
    145–6
research 17–18, 30, 34–5, 107–8
    see also account planners
    creative products 107–8
    managers/agencies 17–18
respect factors 7, 13, 15–16, 27–8,
    105–6, 181
response handling, call centres 15,
    17–18, 147–50, 154
responsibilities
    collaborative partnerships 4–5, 132,
        146–7, 159–60, 168, 181–2
    ownership responsibilities 119
restarts 130–1
retail outlets, visits 17–18
'retainer' fees 137–8
returns, client requirements 5, 7, 13
reviews 47–71, 118, 167, 170–9
    see also evaluations; selection issues
    agencies 47–71, 118, 167, 170–9
    brand effects 51–2
    campaigns 118, 121–2, 170–9
    communications 50, 56, 66–8,
        161–2, 167
    confidentiality issues 50, 56
    decision matrix 51–3
    initial meetings 56
    key considerations 49–54
    lessons learned 167
    low profiles 50, 56
    meetings 56, 172–3
    preparations 49–54
    rumours 54

shortlists 48–9, 56–8, 61–8
third-party specialists 49–52, 54–9
risk-taking considerations 6, 167, 181–2
Rodin, Auguste 99
The Rokeby Venus 99–100, 105
Rolls-Royce 87–8
rumours, agency reviews 54

sales
    budget-setting procedures 144–5
    departments 95
samples 128
Sartre, Jean-Paul 103
'scope creep' 169
scoring matrices, agency evaluations 7–8
secrets 181–2
selection issues
    see also reviews
    agencies 47–71, 143–4, 170–1
    assisted pitches 56–8
    contracts 62–3, 143–4
    decision-making guidelines 62–8
    evolutionary developments 56–8
    face-to-face chemistry 56–8, 68–70
    feedback 65–8, 70–1
    implementation guidelines 62–8
    initial meetings 56
    joint industry guidelines 48–50,
        59–68
    last-minute requests 64
    losers 62–3, 68, 70–1
    low profiles 50, 56
    shortlists 48–9, 56–8, 61–8
    teams 32, 66–71
    third-party specialists 49–52, 54–9,
        139, 153
    trial projects 56–8
    visits 64
    winners 62–3, 68, 70, 143–4, 170–1
    workshops 56–8, 168
    written briefs 50, 56, 59–68
selfless-independence attributes, trusted
    advisers 15–16

senior management, background 33–4, 62–4, 125
sense of belonging, teams 96, 119–20
service level agreements 170–9
shared thinking, benefits 88–90
Sheth, Jagdish N. 13–15
shortlists, agencies 48–9, 56–9, 61–8
signing-off issues
  see also approval...
  milestones 124–5, 128, 164
skills 9–12, 32–3, 34–5, 55, 69–70, 129–32, 146, 160–3
  account planners 34–5
  client services 32–3
  creative-thinking skills 160–3
  diplomacy 131
  'helicopter vision' 146
  internal interviews 9–12
  interpersonal skills 12, 32, 122–3, 131–2, 162–3
  marketing departments 9–12, 131
  organizations 9–12
SMART objectives 85
soap powder commercials 98
Sobel, Andrew 13–16
social side, relationships 163
Speedo 91
standard templates, costs 149–51
standardized evaluations 64–8, 70–1, 97–9, 172–9
Steel, Jon 35, 84
strapline contrasts, propositions 81
strategic planning
  agency evaluation form 179
  campaign development processes 40–2, 120–1, 168–9, 174, 179
  checklist 41, 174, 179
strategic thinking, client requirements 5–8, 52–3, 55, 59–68, 69–70, 103–4, 168–9, 174–9
stress 125, 130

structure factors
  agencies 28–44
  new teams 19–20
success factors 21, 62–3, 68, 70, 91–2, 143–4, 162–3, 167, 170–1, 181–2
support, propositions 87–90
surprise benefits 83–4, 163
synthesis attributes, trusted advisers 16

takeovers *see* mergers...
tasks, objectives 144–5
Tate Modern 99–100
team players, good traits 32
team-building exercises 119–20
teams 9–12, 18–23, 29, 32, 35–6, 40–4, 66–71, 76–92, 118–32, 171–9, 181–2
  communications 9–12, 18–23, 29, 32, 34–5, 66–8, 69–71, 77–92, 119–20, 123–4, 181–2
  core teams 18–23, 171–9
  creative teams 30, 35–6, 42–3, 76–92, 130–1
  dynamics 69–71, 96, 119–24, 159–60
  evaluate-creative benefits 96
  framework factors 19–23
  internal interviews 9–12
  key factors 18–23, 32, 96, 119–20
  new teams 18–23, 40–4, 62–71
  performance issues 21, 170–9
  project management 118–32
  psychometric assessments 20–1, 119
  selection issues 32, 66–71
  sense of belonging 96, 119–20
  team-building exercises 119–20
Tesco 4
tests, production/execution 128, 149
thinking, shared thinking 88–90
third-party specialists 49–52, 54–9, 139, 153
  agency reviews 49–52, 54–9
  main companies 54, 153
'thought leader' agencies 169–70

timescales 38–9, 43–4, 85, 120–32, 147, 164–5, 172
tone of voice (TOV) 81, 101
trade bodies
    agency reviews 48–51, 59–68
    useful information sources 48, 59, 126, 143, 144, 185–6
trade secrets 181–2
traffic role, creative services 38
training needs
    creative training courses 109
    new teams 20–1
transparency needs 5–6, 38, 70–1, 121, 145, 146–7, 181
trial projects, selection issues 56–8
trust 5, 6–7, 12, 13–15, 23, 122–3, 146, 159–60, 162, 166–9, 181
'trusted advisers'
    attributes 15–16
    background 13–16
Truth, Lies and Advertising: The Art of Account Planning (Steel) 35, 84
TV ads 98, 108

Unilever 97
unsolicited messages 51, 77
useful information sources 48, 59, 63–8, 106, 108–9, 126, 143, 144, 185–6

value for money 138–9, 153–4
VAT 149
Victoria & Albert Museum 99

Virgin Atlantic 84
Virgin Mobile 82
vision 6–8, 33, 85, 146
visits, agencies 17–19, 64
visuals 35–6, 42–3, 97, 165–6
von Oech, Roger 109
VW 13

Warhol, Andy 99
'wash-up' meetings 121–2
websites
    budgets 144–5
    production procedures 166
    useful information sources 54, 143, 144, 185–6
where-are-we-now/where-do-we-want-to-be section headings, briefings 79–80
White, Roderick 79
'White Van Men' 86
winners, selection issues 62–3, 68, 70, 143–4, 170–1
win–win guidelines, PBR 140
Work In Progress reports (WIP reports) 151–3
workshops 56–8, 78, 168
world-class people, client requirements 6–8, 55, 69–70, 146–7, 160–3, 170–9
written briefs 50, 56, 59–68, 80

X factor 84